THE ROAD TO DERRY

From The Heritage Commission

The three villages of Derry.

THE ROAD TO
DERRY
A BRIEF HISTORY

RICHARD HOLMES

Charleston London

THE
History
PRESS

Published by The History Press
Charleston, SC 29403
www.historypress.net

First published 2009

Manufactured in the United States

ISBN 978.1.59629.650.3

Library of Congress CIP data applied for.

CONTENTS

PREFACE

While reading a 1916 issue of the *Derry News* I came across an anonymous letter signed "Traveler." The writer was complaining about the condition of the road between Hampstead and Derry. He ended his diatribe with a four-line poem:

It is a toilsome road to Derry,
It is a toilsome way to go,
It's a toilsome way to Derry,
By the roughest road I know.

I immediately thought that the history of Derry has also traveled on a toilsome, rough road. The ancestors of the town struggled against oppression in Ireland and immigrated to America to seek freedom. Here they found that they were mistrusted and unwanted. When finally granted the land called Nutfield, they had to fight others who also claimed the land. In 1738, their church went through a bitter split that divided the town between two pastors. During the Revolutionary War, we were again divided: one of the town's selectmen signed the Declaration of Independence; another selectman was a spy for the British.

Derry separated from Londonderry only after a mean-spirited divorce. Starting in 1870, Derry joined the Industrial Revolution, and we quickly changed from a small agrarian-based community into a town whose main streets were lined with sprawling shoe factories. Within a decade our population doubled as emigrants from Canada, Ireland and eastern Europe rushed into the town. Broadway in the mid-nineteenth century was home to just five families, but within a half century it had grown to resemble a bustling little city with dozens of stores, two trolley lines, many churches, banks, a half-dozen factories, several hotels, restaurants and more. Derry had become the boomtown of this part of New Hampshire.

All this prosperity would come to a crashing halt with the Great Depression. Five of our six shoe factories closed, and many of our families went on welfare as our unemployment spiked to about 30 percent. It was said that Derry was hit worse by the Depression than any other town in the state. The town would not really recover until 1963, when interstate highway I-93 opened. Suddenly, our population began to double and redouble. In less than two generations, the town's population had grown nearly fivefold. During the last forty-five years Derry has gone through three different forms of government, fifteen different town administrators and a secessionist movement in East Derry. The council meetings have been too often filled with petty bickering, rancor and derision. These televised meetings are locally referred to as the "Tuesday night fights." At the last local election, less than a tenth of our registered voters bothered to go to the polls.

Through all these struggles Derry has been the home to thousands of good, hardworking citizens who have worked tirelessly to try and make the town into a community. Also during the nearly three centuries of Derry's history, many famous men and women have called it home. There have been those from Derry who achieved fame in nearly every aspect of public life. Few towns have had such citizens as General John Stark, Major Robert Rogers, spy Stephen Holland, Patriot Matthew Thornton, educator Mary Lyon, poet Robert Frost, singer Buddy Stewart, scientist Walter Adams, Olympian Trisha Dunn, TV personality Samantha Brown, murderer Pamela Smart and astronaut Alan Shepard Jr.

Today the town promotes itself as "New Hampshire's place to be." This may be true, but it has been a long toilsome road to get to where it is today. This book is intended to be a very brief history to help the nonhistorian better understand the road to today's Derry. It is my hope that this history gives our residents a sense of pride in their community and helps guide the town's future by knowing about its past. This book has had to compact nearly three hundred years of history into a relatively short book; it does not purport to tell the whole story. For more in-depth reading, the reader would be well served by exploring the historical collections in our two public libraries or our town's museum.

A quick thanks to the many local people who have guided me in writing this book and helped me to avoid making too many dumb mistakes when reporting the recent past. Of particular help has been the reference desk of the Derry Public Library, the members of the Heritage Commission, the many town officials both past and present who answered my queries, photographer David Fuccillo, computer specialist Doug Rathburn, photo-restorer Walter Chapman, Lois Dugan, artist Rosaline Hartley, the *Derry News* and especially my wife Carol; children John, Leah, Julianne and Andrew; and grandchildren Jacob, Christopher and Jeffrey for allowing me the time to write this book.

CHAPTER 1

THE ARRIVAL FROM EUROPE

The events that led to the founding of Derry began in seventeenth-century Scotland when the England put down an insurrection in Northern Ireland. The confiscated Ulster Plantation was given out to London merchants thinking it would be easier to control if the native Irish were kicked off their farms. The word was passed to Scotland that rich farmland was available at very cheap rents. Soon thousands were leaving Scotland and crossing the Irish Sea to Ulster. They brought to Ireland their pride in being Scottish, their skill as weavers and their Presbyterian faith.

At first, life in Ulster was good. The land was fertile, and the Scots made a comfortable living growing flax and weaving linen. This good life ended in 1689 when the native Irish aided by the French rose up in rebellion. Thousands of the Scots took refuge behind the thick walls of the city of Londonderry. There for months, the Scots suffered starvation during the siege of the city. Finally on the 105th day of the siege, young Jamie McGregor, high atop the Londonderry Cathedral, saw that a British warship had broken through the barriers on the River Foyle. Young McGregor immediately fired a cannon to let the city know that the siege was over. In time, this boy would become the leader of the Nutfield colony.

The years that followed were hard on the Ulster Presbyterians. The established church was the Anglican Church of England, and the government in London viewed the Scots and their Presbyterian faith as inferior. Soon royal edicts were enforced that forbade Scots from teaching school or holding most public offices. Presbyterian ministers couldn't serve communion, and the marriages they had performed were considered invalid. Most of their churches were seized and given to Anglican clerics. In addition, the Presbyterians were greatly upset by the "farmers of tithes" that the Crown sent out to collect a 10 percent income tax to support the Church of England.

During the early years of the eighteenth century, the quality of life began to decline even further: smallpox epidemics killed many Scots; the British Parliament passed laws restricting the sale of linen from Ulster; rumors were spreading that the king was going to double the rent on their land; and some Scots were being kicked off their rented farms so the land could be leased to native Irishmen. To many Ulstermen this seemed like a good time to leave Ireland, and they speculated that the New World might give their families a better life. Word had recently come from New England that the Presbyterians would be welcomed in Boston.

Soon in Ulster there was a "fever for immigration." The first to put these dreams into action was the Reverend James McGregor (1677–1729). He was the pastor of a small Presbyterian church in the tiny village of Aghadowey in county Londonderry. In the village he was known as the "peacemaker." He and his wife Maryanne were the parents of ten children and very poor. Fortunately, his congregation included a few wealthy landowners, notably his father-in-law Elder David Cargill and brothers-in-law James McKeen, Esq., and Captain James Gregg. It is believed that these three helped finance the sea passage to the New World.

After much prayer, the entire Aghadowey congregation voted to follow their pastor to America. Before departing, McGregor preached from Exodus: "If Thy presence goes not with me, carry us not up hence." In this sermon he also preached that they must say farewell to friends, relations and their native land in order to find economic, political, cultural and religious freedoms. In the next few decades, thousands of Ulster Scots would follow the lead of the congregation of Aghadowey to make similar pilgrimages for freedom. *The Encyclopedia of the Irish in America* calls Reverend James McGregor the "Moses of the Scotch Irish in America."

On August 4, 1718, the brigantine *Robert* arrived in Boston Harbor with McGregor and the sixteen families of his congregation. Other Ulster Scots had come to America before, but these were the first who had pledged to stay together. In Boston, however, the population was English with little tolerance for the newcomers. They viewed the Scots as being social inferiors who dressed strangely and had bad hygienic practices. It was reported that at the dinner table the Ulstermen spread butter on their bread with their thumbs.

Most Bostonians belonged to the Congregational or Anglican Church and believed that these emigrants from Ireland must be Irish and thus members of the Catholic Church. Pastor McGregor in disgust wrote to Governor Shute to protest being termed "Irish." He argued that they were Scots who came originally from the island of Britain but had been living in

Reverend James McGregor and his family leave Aghadowey, Northern Ireland, for the New World in 1718. *Illustration by Rosalind Giuffrida Hartley.*

Ireland. Some locals bought guns to protect themselves from these strange-appearing newcomers and feared that they would soon "eat them out of house and home." The Scots were anxious to leave Boston—but where to go? McGregor was forced to take a temporary preaching post in Dracut, Massachusetts, until a land grant could be acquired.

In the fall of 1718, Governor Samuel Shute persuaded most of the Scots to start a settlement in Casco Bay, Maine. Here they suffered in frozen misery during the winter of 1718–19. They had too little food and only the most rudimentary shelters to protect them from the harsh Maine winter. In December, the governor was forced to send a hundred bushels of corn to feed these shivering, hungry emigrants. In the spring, the Scots voted to return to Boston to beg Shute to find them a more hospitable site for their settlement. On the way back from Maine, they heard about an unoccupied piece of land called Nutfield. It was given that name because people from the coast had gone there for decades to gather feed for their livestock. In Nutfield there were thousands of oak, butternut and chestnut trees that would yield countless bushels of nuts and huge marshlands covered with hay. The Scots sailed up the Merrimack River as far as Haverhill to investigate the suitability of Nutfield as their new home.

James McKeen and James Gregg led the men fourteen miles through the wilderness and found that Nutfield was indeed to their liking. Quickly the men built crude log cabins near a stream that they called "the West Running Brook" and then went back to the ship at Haverhill. A crowd of Haverhill men gathered at the dock to watch the Ulster women and children being rowed in from their ship. Undoubtedly most of the locals were very relieved that the Ulster families had decided not to remain in Haverhill. Suddenly, without warning, the rowboat tipped over, throwing the passengers into the river. Immediately, according to Bolton's *Scotch Irish Pioneers in Ulster and America*, the men of Haverhill cheered, and a song was composed about the women and children of Aghadowey:

> *They then began to scream and bawl,*
> *And if the Devil had spread his net,*
> *He would have made a glorious haul.*

Doubtlessly that night this anti-Scot ditty was sung with gusto at the taverns of Haverhill.

A team of men was immediately dispatched to Dracut to ask Reverend James McGregor to join them in Nutfield. He accepted, and on April 12, 1719, by Beaver Lake, he preached his first sermon in Nutfield. The theme was taken from Ezekiel 32:2, which asks God to provide "a hiding place from the winds and a covert from the tempest; as rivers of water in a dry place; as the shadow of a great rock in a weary land." Immediately, the pioneers began clearing a "common field near the West Running Brook." Here they would plant the first crop of potatoes in British America. Not having enough food that first winter, they followed the suggestion of an old Indian called Ezekiel and caught shad, salmon and eels at the Amoskeag Falls on the Merrimack River.

Originally, Shute had promised McGregor's congregation a grant of 144 square miles, but by the time the settlers arrived, it had shrunk as the towns of Chester, Litchfield and Nashua claimed some of the land. In addition, the Massachusetts towns of Haverhill, Salem and Newbury thought that parts of the Nutfield grant were really theirs. As proof, they had a deed signed by an Indian named John. For years, the Haverhill authorities would kidnap Nutfield's farmers for trespassing on their land. To add to the Scots' problems, it turns out Nutfield was really located in New Hampshire, not Massachusetts. To clear up their title, the Nutfield pioneers got a deed to the land from Colonel John Wheelwright whose grandfather had purchased the land from Chief Passaconaway in 1629. To get the tract regranted by New Hampshire, the Nutfield settlers resorted to the age-old practice of bribery. Lieutenant Governor John Wentworth was made a gift of a 120-acre home lot near Beaver Lake and 500 additional acres where he "shall think fit." Other Portsmouth politicos were given similar tokens of "appreciation."

Soon the population of the Nutfield colony began to grow as word of the success of the Aghadowey colonists spread through Northern Ireland. In 1720, the settlers began to petition the New Hampshire government for a town charter. More bribes were sent out to the Boston and Portsmouth bigwigs, and a fawning letter was sent to Lieutenant Governor John Wentworth praising him as their "patron and guardian." On June 21, 1722, Nutfield received its charter, signed by Governor Shute of Massachusetts and Lieutenant Governor John Wentworth of New Hampshire on behalf of King George I of Great Britain. The new town took the official name of Londonderry, after the Northern Ireland county from where the Aghadowey pioneers had emigrated in 1718. The charter specified the following provisions:

1. *Each of the town's proprietors had to pay their taxes, build a house within three years and settle a family in that house. They must also clear three acres of land within four years. If a proprietor failed to satisfy these obligations he would lose his land.*
2. *A meetinghouse had to be built within four years.*

Reverend David McGregor (1709–77), the son of the leader of the Nutfield pioneers and the town's first teacher. *Illustration by Rosalind Giuffrida Hartley.*

3. *Each year in October a peck of potatoes must be sent to the royal governor as a token rent.*
4. *No one could cut down trees that were of sufficient size to be used for ships' masts.*
5. *A town fair could be held every May and October and a market day every Wednesday.*
6. *A town meeting will be held every March.*

In the event of an Indian War, the first two provisions could be postponed until four years after the onset of peace.

Initially, in 1720, the land had divided into 105 house lots of 60 acres each. With the town charter of 1722, the ownership in the remaining land was divided into 132.5 shares. When any land was sold, the shareholders would be given a percentage of the sale price. The largest shareholder was Reverend James McGregor, who was awarded 3 shares plus a half share for a servant. He also got a special bonus of 250 acres. The Wentworth family received 2 shares plus 360 acres. Some land was, of course, better than other land. To appraise the land fairly, John Stuart's 60-acre Lane Road home lot was declared to be the "Precept Farm." Land that was judged to be of poorer quality than Stuart's was sold at a lower price; land that was better than the Precept Farm was sold at a higher price. In addition, several farms were exempt from taxes because their owners had been at the 1689 siege of Londonderry. Each home lot owner was also given enough meadowland to annually "yield three small loads of hay."

The town, in time, would be divided into a number of sections called ranges. The first laid out was the Double Range, where in 1719 the initial settlement had been made. Here the pioneers had built their log cabin within sight of one another because of the fear of an Indian attack. As more and more settlers moved into Londonderry, the proprietors sent surveyors to lay out other ranges named after their location or original settlers. Derry Village was mainly in Aikens Range; West Derry in Eayers Range and English Range was settled by non-Scots. These range lots were poorly surveyed, and this would later result in countless lawsuits.

With each passing year, Londonderry grew larger in population. By the mid-eighteenth century it was the second-largest town in New Hampshire with only the capital city of Portsmouth being larger. The 114 square miles of Londonderry would, however, not remain intact for long. Soon pieces would begin to break off to become new towns. The southeast corner of old Nutfield was separated in 1741 to become the town of Windham. The northwest corner became Derryfield in 1751 (now the city of Manchester). The southwest corner became Hudson in 1778. By 1800, all that was left of the original 1719 grant was just 78 square miles. In 1827 those would be divided into the present towns of Derry and Londonderry.

CHAPTER 2

POLITICS

The first town meeting in Nutfield was held on November 9, 1719, and a committee of seven men was elected as a "committee to manage the public affairs of the town." It would not be until 1722 that they were renamed as selectmen. There were also a number of elected positions back then that are unfamiliar today: hog reeves were supposed to keep pigs out of the neighbor's garden; tithing men were to enforce moral laws, such as the laws concerning Sunday travel, and carried as a badge of the office a black rod with a pewter knob; haywards were to keep cows and horses out of the public land; sealers were to check on the quality of locally produced products; and fence viewers were to rule on land disputes.

The town meeting form of government would remain in place for the next 266 years. Each year the selectmen would post the warrant giving the date of the town meeting, stating how much money the town wanted to spend during the next fiscal year, what officers were to be elected and what special projects were proposed for the next year. At first, the town meetings were held at the meetinghouse on East Derry Hill. After 1738, the town was divided into an east and west parish, and the town meetings were frequently alternated between their two meetinghouses. While both parishes were part of the town of Londonderry, they each supported their own meetinghouse and paid for preaching out of tax dollars collected only within their own parish.

The dividing line between the east and west parishes was roughly a north–south line that runs along today's Bypass Route 28. The east parish was the more affluent. Here was located the largest meetinghouse and the homes of the majority of the town's doctors, lawyers and merchants. Since at least 1738, it had been called the "Derry Parish of Londonderry." The other parish was called "the Londonderry Parish of Londonderry" and was more rural. From the beginning of the town, most of the elected town officers lived in the Derry Parish. That is just the way it was. The east-side men thought of themselves as being better educated and better able to run the town. The west-side men were thought of as being just a bunch of farmers.

Starting in 1825, the men of the west parish began to vote as a bloc at town meeting and defeated a number of candidates from the Derry Parish. This greatly upset the men of the east. Something had to be done! A cabal led by Alanson Tucker, James Thom and John Porter secretly plotted the fate of the town. In March 1827, when the warrant was posted on the tavern door, an article submitted by petition was included. It proposed to separate the Derry Parish from Londonderry to make it a separate town. If this wasn't bad enough, the boundary of the new town was not going to be the old parish line. Instead, the line was to be located a mile farther west; Tucker, Thom and Porter of the east parish were, in effect, stealing several thousand acres of land that had always been in the west parish.

State law said that a town couldn't just be split in half. Only the state government could incorporate a new town. Londonderry in 1827 was allowed to elect three members to the state legislature. The westerners' idea was to have the town meeting send only one representative, and by voting as a bloc they could elect the popular John Miltimore to the legislature. It was well known that Miltimore was opposed to the split. With Miltimore as the only representative, there'd be no one to introduce the succession bill in the legislature. At the town meeting held at the First Parish Church, all went as planned and Miltimore was elected. By now, it was getting dark, so it was moved to adjourn the meeting to another day. With this, most of the westerners quickly left to start the long walk home.

As soon as most of the men of the west had left, the east-side gang reconvened the meeting and voted to reconsider the vote on sending only one representative. Because it was dark, the moderator called for candles to be lit so the votes could be counted. The few westerners who remained in the hall tried to stop the count by using horsewhips to snap out the candle flames. This effort failed, and Alanson Tucker and John Porter were elected to the legislature. The meeting was then adjourned. The next week the second session of the town meeting voted 303 to 253 not to split the town. That vote, of course, didn't really matter because Tucker and Porter had gone to Concord and persuaded the House and Senate to approve the division. Governor Benjamin Pierce signed the bill on July 2, 1827. The new town had been born.

The new town took Derry as its name. This was actually the original name of Londonderry in Northern Ireland. In Gaelic, Doire (Derry) meant "oak woods." The new town of Derry, New Hampshire, had a population of about 2,200 inhabitants with a land area of about thirty-six square miles. This translated into population density of about 61 people per square mile. In 2009, the population density is nearly 1,000 people per square mile.

Derry's first town meeting was held at the First Parish Church on July 18, 1827. The men then proceeded to elect one moderator, one clerk, five selectmen, one treasurer, three auditors, twenty-six highway supervisors, five fence viewers, four corders of wood, five cullers of staves, eight hog reeves, one pound keeper, one sealer of weights and measures, four constables and five members of the school board. That year it cost $1,500 to run the town. Taxes were given a 6 percent discount if paid by September 6. In 1831, the office of tax collector was auctioned off to the lowest bidder. The winner was Samuel Adams with a bid that he would do the job for 1 percent of all money he collected. The most unusual town office ever elected was that of "Chairman of the Board of Hog Reeves." It was given in 1831 to attorney Thornton Benton, who had a local reputation of being a "schemer."

Derry would not have an official town hall until 1876 with the construction of the Upper Village Hall in East Derry. It served as the town hall, library, jail and social hall until 1905, when the Benjamin Adams Memorial Building was built on East Broadway. In 1972, the old post office on East Broadway became the new town hall. This building soon became very overcrowded, and in 2001 the Derry Municipal Center was built on Manning Street.

During the nineteenth century, the town meetings were fairly unchanged from those that were held in 1722. Only men could vote, so few women attended. After a prayer by a local preacher would come the election of officers, the discussion and the voting on the budget and special warrant articles. While only those who had reached their twenty-first birthday could vote, the back of the room was usually filled with boys and teenagers in awe as the town fathers gave pious orations on matters political. Probably even more exciting to them, however, were the red-faced arguments that often broke into fistfights.

During the town meetings, the moderator was an absolute monarch whose word was law. Judge George Grinnell used to tell this story from the 1940s, when he was town moderator. During the town meeting, he heard a loud voice from the balcony questioning the "integrity" of one of his rulings. The critic turned out to be Red Lambert—a perpetual thorn in the side of most local politicos. Red was also blessed with a very loud voice. Moderator Grinnell started to steam and turned the gavel over to an assistant. He flew up the stairs at a run and gave Lambert a "knuckle sandwich then grabbed Lambert by the scruff of the neck and seat of the pants, throwing him down the stairs. Fortunately, Red grabbed the handrail and didn't fall all the way down." George later told the author, "I thought I killed him…the handrail saved me from going to jail."

Some votes were won by methods more foul than fair. A swig of whiskey, a "word to the wise" by one's employer or a dollar quickly slipped into a hand would frequently help change a voter's mind. About 1900, Rosecrans Pillsbury thought that he could influence a vote by letting the men in his shoe factory leave work early, giving them each a trolley ticket to the town hall in East Derry and telling them how they should vote. The Shepard family, who owned the trolley company, was on the opposite political side from the Pillsburys. Fred Shepard heard about Rose's plan to stuff the ballot box with shoe workers' votes. As the passenger-loaded trolley started to climb East Derry Hill, it suddenly took a sharp left turn and went into the trolley repair barn. Young Bart Shepard immediately locked the barn door, trapping all the shoe workers inside. The barn door wasn't unlocked until after the polls were declared closed.

Despite the fact that women couldn't vote, it was theorized that the ladies voted indirectly through their husbands and fathers. By tradition, females were not even allowed to speak at town meetings, probably because of St. Paul's command in First Corinthians 14:33 that "women should remain silent in the church." The first Derry women mentioned in a town election were Nancy Danforth and Rebecca Montgomery in 1837, who each received two write-in votes for governor. Today their candidacy is a mystery; perhaps it was meant as a joke or as criticism of the regular candidate—or maybe the four men did think that these ladies were qualified to lead the state.

It wouldn't be until 1857 that women were again cited in the town records. In that year, a warrant article called on the town not to hire any unmarried men unless they publicly explained why they were "remaining in a state of celibacy." The second part of the proposal requested that "mothers, wives and daughters of the town" attend all public meetings to "aid by their prayers, presence and other kindly ministries to those who bear the ark of religion, liberties, independence and everlasting freedom." The article was dismissed by the all-male voters as "frivolous and unconstitutional."

It would not be until 1872 that the state allowed women to hold any elected town office. While women couldn't be a selectman or town clerk, they could vote in school elections and be selected as member of the school board. In 1873, Miss Emma Shute, age thirty-three, was elected a member of the prudential committee of the Ryan's Hill school district. She was not reelected the next year as the board went back to being all male until 1878, when another woman was elected to the board. In 1886, a local reporter said that Susan B. Anthony's crusade for women's suffrage apparently had little effect in Derry because "less than a dozen of our ladies availed themselves of the opportunity to vote."

Starting in 1902, the drive for women's suffrage became stronger in Derry when Miss Mary Chase gave a series of lectures on the rights of women. She said in a *Derry News* article, "All bad men as a rule were opposed to women's suffrage." She acknowledged that there were some "good men" who were also anti-suffrage, but once they saw who was on the ladies' side, they would change their position. Derry storekeeper Leonard Pillsbury declared emphatically that "taxation without representation by women is tyranny."

The leading opponent of women's suffrage was factory owner Rosecrans Pillsbury. In the state legislature he declared that "women should remain on the pedestal where we have always worshipped them." Also opposed was Mrs. Anne B. Shepard, who led a statewide women's organization that was opposed to giving females the franchise. Interestingly enough, after women did get the vote, Shepard became very active in politics. In 1924, she was a member of the Electoral College pledged to President Calvin Coolidge. She was the first president of New Hampshire Federation of Women's Clubs, state regent of the Daughters of the American Revolution (DAR) and New England chairman of the War Victory Committee during World War I. She was the grandmother of astronaut Alan Shepard Jr.

The Nineteenth Amendment to the U.S. Constitution was passed in 1919, giving women the right to vote. On November 2, 1920, women cast their first votes in Derry. In preparation, the town clerk printed two checklists of registered voters. One list contained the names of 1,645 men and the other, 1,057 women. The polls opened at 10:05 a.m., and despite being a rainy day, there was already a line of voters at the door of the Adams Memorial Building. The first woman to vote was Emma Horne, the fifty-four-year-old wife of Headmaster Perley Horne of Pinkerton Academy. While we don't know how Emma voted, the Republicans did sweep the election in Derry, helping to send Warren Harding to the White House.

The first woman to be elected a town officer was Nellie Wood, who in 1924 became a supervisor of the checklist. It would not be until 1976 that we had a woman in the top town office. In that year, Janet Conroy, a forty-four-year-old mother of four, was elected as selectman. She had previously been president of the Floyd School Parent-Teacher Association and a columnist for the *Derry News*. Her politically themed poetry was published under the nom de plume of the "High Street Hack." In 1979, she was unanimously selected as chairman of the board of selectmen. In 1988, she became the first woman to belong to the Derry Village Rotary Club. That same year,

Vickie Buckley Chase became the first woman member of the town's other Rotary Club.

In more recent times, there have been women in elected office in Derry. In 1986, Phyllis Katsakiores was Derry's first town councilor and has served many years in the state legislature. Gladys Downing was elected town clerk in 1949 and tax collector in 1957. Cecile Hoisington served as town clerk from 1967 to 1990. Marion Pounder was chosen as the first trustee of Pinkerton Academy in 1977. To date the longest-serving town administrator was Carol Granville, who led the office for over five years.

The Republican Party was established in 1854, and since that time the voters of Derry have been almost always loyal to the Grand Old Party. In 1912, the town voted Democratic, but that was because the Republican Party had been split into the "Regular Republicans" led by President Taft and the "Progressive Bull Moose Republicans" led by former president Theodore Roosevelt. The vote was Taft 348, Roosevelt 186 and Democratic candidate Woodrow Wilson, 495. If the Republicans had voted for a single candidate, they would have seized the victory. In 1916, the Democrats proved that they really could win in a two-candidate race. Wilson won reelection with a local vote of 725 to 547 over Republican Charles Hughes. The Democrats celebrated with a parade and a "jollification" at the Opera House with 700 celebrants. The next presidential election saw "normalcy" return to Derry when the town voted for Republican Warren Harding over Democrat James Cox by a vote of 1,375 to 897.

In the presidential elections of 1924 and 1928, Derry remained loyal to the GOP. The election of 1932 would be different. The Great Depression was devastating the economy of the town. Derry's shoe factories and banks were threatening to close, and local families were going on welfare. In March, James Roosevelt spoke at a Derry rally, saying how his father, Franklin Delano Roosevelt, would give America a new economic deal, as well as putting an end to Prohibition. Roosevelt defeated Republican Herbert Hoover 1,326 to 1,319. The Republican Party would win the next nineteen consecutive presidential elections.

Up until the 1940s, the budget proposed by the selectmen was voted up or down at the annual town meeting. In 1943, the town began having an appointed budget committee. A fiscally conservative moderator would appoint like-minded budget committee members, and a more moderate moderator would select members who would be more apt to approve spending for new town projects. Under the state's Municipal Budget Act, the budget committee had a nearly complete veto over all aspects of the town's budget. If the selectmen proposed spending $1 million on roads, the budget committee might approve only $500,000. The voters were powerless to overrule the budget committee except by 10 percent. Thus the most the town could spend on roads that year was $500,000, plus an additional 10 percent for a total of $550,000. The budget committee could even vote zero dollars for a warrant article of which they disapproved, in effect killing the proposed project before it was even put to a vote. In 1975, the budget committee became an elected office.

Relations between the selectmen and budget committee really got testy in 1976 when it was discovered that the Water Commissioner, Mark MacDermott, had embezzled $142,000. After a series of clandestine meetings, the budget committee decided to begin impeachment proceedings against Town Administrator Frank Carlton and Selectmen Ernest Gaines and Frederick Tompkins. The committee charged that the three had "failed to comply with regulations regarding budget appropriations" and had not been prudent in detecting and preventing the theft.

The removal trial began in October 1976 at the Rockingham County Superior Court in Exeter. After three days of testimony, the judge recommended that the two boards "iron out" their problems back in Derry. The next week, at a crowded public meeting, the budget committee indicated its willingness to drop its charges against the selectmen and the town administrator. This capitulation upset the budget board's lawyer, who said that the board would waste $12,000 in legal fees if it didn't continue the fight. The lawyer also said that if Carlton were found guilty, the bonding company would have to pay back the money that MacDermott had stolen. The lawyer for the selectmen and administrator also pushed to continue the fight so that they could clear their good names.

In early November 1977, the budget committee did drop the case, but the administrator and the selectmen asked the court to continue the case. The judge thought that he could satisfy both parties by issuing a consent agreement to deal with future "financial disputes." While the selectmen and administrator accepted this document, the budget committee rejected it because the selectmen and administrator didn't admit their guilt in the mismanagement of funds. In August 1977, the judge ordered both sides to sit down and settle things once and for all. This did not happen and the case went to court. By now, the legal fees were in excess of $50,000.

The Derry trial lasted three days, and the decision came down five months later. After two years of expensive litigations, the judge ruled against the budget committee. In his ruling, the jurist said that the managing of town funds was as much the responsibility of the budget committee as it was the selectmen's. The case was over but the bitter feelings continued.

Many on both sides were beginning to see Derry government as being somewhat dysfunctional and operating in an environment where civility and compromise was impossible. The *Derry News* classified the local political environment as being in a "quagmire."

In 1981, the selectmen's proposed budget was $4.9 million, and the budget committee cut this figure by 17 percent. This so infuriated the selectmen that they put on the ballot an article to strip the budget committee of its power to control spending. Town Administrator Carlton warned the voters that the committee's budget would force streetlights to be turned off and snowplowing reduced. The voters did vote to restore 10 percent to the town's budget, but defeated the call to hobble the budget committee. May Casten, the conservative leader of the budget committee, publicly admonished the selectmen to "stop playing politics." The selectmen retorted that they had to do what was in the best interest of the town and not just the taxpayers.

The next year the budget committee axed the budget by 25 percent and eliminated many items such as spraying for gypsy moths and redesigning the dump that was believed to be polluting the area's groundwater. The committee also voted zero dollars to pay the salary of the town administrator.

Those taxpayers whose property tax bills increased by over $1,000 raise their hands during a 1995 protest by the Derry Taxpayers Association. *Photo by Josh Reynolds,* Derry News.

This action might have been brought about because the administrator had just proposed a 39.45 percent tax increase. Now the town government had less money than the town thought it needed and lacked a town administrator to run the daily operations of the town. After the vote, Selectman Janet Conroy discouragingly predicted in the *Derry News*, "This is going to be one hell of a year."

As the town grew larger, its problems grew more complicated. Most citizens lacked the commitment, time or skill to fully understand the complexities of running a town the size of Derry. Each year there were fewer and fewer voters who would show up for the town meeting. Most of the printed town reports were unread. One year in the 1980s, the town meeting lasted for five days, and at the last session there were only eighty-seven people present and voting.

On November 6, 1984, the voters decided to change the structure of Derry's government. They voted 3,113 to 2,593 to approve a charter drafted by a committee led by Frederick Tompkins. Derry would have a part-time mayor—paid $15,000 per year—who would be responsible for preparing the budget and presiding over council meetings. He was also given the power to remove all board and commission members. The town administrator would run the daily business of the town and would serve at the pleasure of the mayor. The council would serve as the legislative body of the town. With this vote, the town meetings, selectmen and budget committee were no more.

The last town meeting was held at Grinnell School on Saturday, March 15, 1985. There were five hundred voters in attendance, as well as rows of reporters and television cameras to record the last act in the political theatre that had begun in 1719. At the end of the daylong session, May Casten made the motion to adjourn the meeting. Eunice Campbell seconded this. Selectman Janet Conroy immediately thanked the crowd for staying to "the bitter end." The motion passed by a unanimous vote, and everyone went home.

During the next seven years, Derry would have three mayors—Paul Collette (1985–89), John Dowd (1989–92) and May Casten (1992–93). Each of the mayors had their own style of administration, and in hindsight, it can be said that each tried to watch out for the best interest of the town—as they saw it. Collette and Dowd were moderate centrist Republicans, while Casten was cut from a different cloth and came to office in a time of economic recession.

May Casten was an extreme fiscal conservative who was very approachable by her constituents. She had been appointed to many town boards and elected selectman, and was councilor and even queen of the 1939 Derry

The three mayors of Derry: John Dowd (left), Paul Collette and May Casten (inset). Derry News *photo.*

Winter Carnival. She was a founder of the Derry Taxpayers Association. She and her equally flamboyant twin sister, Millie DiMarzio, were known around town as the Gold Dust Twins. It could always be said of May that she remembered who her friends were. The inverse of that comment was equally true. The first words she said after her election as mayor was to former Mayor Dowd: "Give me the keys to the castle!" Many loved her candor, but others believed that her antics during the televised council meetings were an embarrassment for the town. To many, she was a valiant warrior doing battle to control the town's budget; others saw May as an ill-prepared populist whose administrative style resulted in mismanagement and confusion.

In March 1993, the town voted 2,094 to 954 to end the seven-year experiment with a mayor-council form of government. In its place would be a seven-member council. This government structure is still in place, but there is at present a new charter commission to reexamine how Derry is governed. Some of its proponents advocate a city government for Derry. The leaders of this effort believe that such a change will help rein in our taxes. Others, however, question if Derry really has a "tax problem." They argue that if the people were really concerned about taxes, they would have voted in the town's election. In the council election of March 2009, only about 8 percent of the registered voters bothered to cast their ballot. Sad!

Perhaps the most divisive political action in recent years was the movement to have East Derry break away from the town of Derry. For decades, there had been contention over the boundaries of the East Derry Fire District (EDFD). Many in East Derry thought the Derry Fire District (DFD) had clandestinely expanded its territory, thus robbing the EDFD of much of its tax base. In April 1977, at the annual meeting of the EDFD, William Cassidy proposed looking into "whether or not it would be feasible for East Derry to secede from Derry and establish its own township." Nothing was apparently done on the proposal, and it seems to have died from lack of interest.

The year 2002 was a tough one for Derry. Taxes were rising, the schools were overcrowded and the town's unemployment rate was 25 percent higher that the state's average. In April, the East Derry Citizens Committee was formed to see if it was viable for East Derry to become a town. The next month, committee leader June Fahey announced that they had crunched the numbers and found that it would indeed work; East Derry represented 30 percent of the property value of the entire town. In addition, East Derry already had its own post office, fire department, library, cemetery and elementary school. Its town hall would be the stately Upper Village Hall. The boundary of the new town would be that of the EDFD.

The secessionists' committee held regular meetings and issued many press releases. Soon everyone in town was talking about the Derry–East Derry split, but few publicly supported its goals. Early in 2003, Derry United was formed to keep Derry as one town. A petition was circulated to "stop the assault on the town." Just like in 1827, no town could be formed without the approval of the state legislature, and ten of the town's representatives signed a letter opposed to the breakup. Only Representative Ron Dupuis, a leader in the pro-split committee, declined to sign.

On February 10, 2003, a legislative hearing was held in Concord before the committee on Municipal and County Government regarding House Bill 399—the East Derry secession bill. The room was filled mainly with those who were testifying in opposition of the bill; its supporters were few in number. The next month the bill was declared "inexpedient to legislate." It was dead and nearly everyone in town was happy. In July, Ron Dupuis moved out of town, saying he "couldn't afford to live here." Also in 2003, June Fahey lost her bid to be elected to the town council.

The position of Derry's town administrator does not have much job security. The town meetings had created the office of town administrator or manager on three separate occasions: 1949, 1964 and 1973. The town meetings also voted to eliminate the office on three occasions: 1953, 1965 and 1982. Gary Stenhouse, the current administrator, is the eighteenth

Conservationist Albert Doolittle signs in as being opposed to East Derry splitting off from Derry in a 2003 legislative hearing in Concord. Waiting to sign is Paul Dionne and Ginny True. Derry legislator Kenneth Gould watches at the left.

person to hold this position. There have also been at least six individuals who have served as acting or interim town administrators. The average town administrator remains in Derry for about two years, though one lasted only about nine months and another survived just over five years.

A few of these town administrators quit Derry on their own accord to seek more lucrative employment. Some others left to escape from the maelstrom's whirl that is Derry politics. The town administrator can be fired for pretty much any reason. One administrator was discharged because he said some unkind things about the mayor's wife during a very public mayor-administrator screaming match. A number of departing administrators have expressed a sense of great relief upon leaving Derry and looked forward to more peaceful employment elsewhere.

CHAPTER 3

SCHOOLS

Education was important to the early settlers of Nutfield as it was felt that it was a holy obligation to see that children could read. Without knowledge of scripture, the old deluder Satan would surely snare the unwary into his net of lies. Also without book learning, legal contracts and deeds couldn't be understood, and big men could take advantage of the ill educated. Perhaps schooling was also the more precious because it had been denied to them for so long in Northern Ireland.

In 1725, the town voted to build a grammar school near the site of the present Taylor Library. It was built of logs and measured twelve by eighteen feet with seven-foot-high walls and fireplaces at both ends. The nearby meetinghouse was unheated, so it's likely that this school doubled as a warming station between morning and afternoon church services in the winter. There is no record of the town buying any school furniture or supplies so the scholars likely sat on roughly constructed benches and wrote their letters on pieces of wood or birch bark. The Bible was probably their only textbook as it is unlikely that these impoverished early settlers could afford hornbooks or the New England Primer.

The first teacher on record was David McGregor in 1725; he was the son of the pastor/founder of the town and had been home taught by his father. The second teacher was John Herby, who was paid thirty-six pounds per year. In 1729, Reverend Matthew Clark was paid eighty pounds per year to preach and an additional forty pounds if he would "save our town from keeping any other grammar school master." This meant that all the town's children would have to travel to East Derry if their parents wanted them schooled. It was likely that most children from the outlying area were educated by their parents or neighbors.

It wouldn't be until 1732 that the town voted to have two schools. Both schools would receive equal funding and be open for an equal length of time. While the records are silent on the actual length of the school year, it likely didn't exceed a couple of months per year. Such rudimentary education would be sufficient for boys who would grow up to be farmers and girls who would likely be housewives. Few locals would need any kind of advanced education. During the entire eighteenth century, there were only twenty men from town who were known to have graduated from college. Most who wanted to pursue a professional career would apprentice with a master in the desired field of study. Future general John Sullivan learned law by studying at the home of Attorney General Samuel Livermore in East Derry. Dr. Nathan Plummer studied medicine with local physician Robert Bartley.

It would not be until after the Revolutionary War that locals began to see the need for more advanced learning than could be acquired in the local schools. In 1793, a group of local men hired Zephaniah Swift Moore, the future president of both Williams and Amherst Colleges, to start a secondary school in town. The Classical High School was located just east of the First Parish Church. It was hoped that tuition from area students would sustain the cost of running the school. The school was apparently never a roaring success and closed in 1814.

During the nineteenth century the town would be subdivided into ten school districts, each with its own schoolhouse. By having multiple districts, the schoolhouse was an easy walk from most students' homes. Each district would vote annually on how much money it would tax its residents for support of the school. The more affluent the district, the larger the appropriation would usually be. The citizens in the Island Pond district were mainly hardscrabble farmers. In 1856, they voted only enough money to provide for eleven weeks of schooling that year. The taxpayers in Derry Village were more apt to be upper middle class as it was home to many doctors, lawyers, merchants and factory owners. That year they voted that their children should have thirty-one weeks of school. After 1886, the town was made into a single school district with equal funding.

The affluent East Derry and Derry Village districts each had well-built brick schoolhouses that were warm in the winter and cool in the summer. By contrast, the rural districts' schools were often small, primitive, drafty hovels that were uncomfortable at all times of the year. A fireplace heated them that burned wood brought in by the locals, who were allowed to pay off their school tax with firewood. Too often this wood was green and made the school's interior very smoky. In addition, the rural schools had few windows and lamps so they were usually dark and gloomy. Too many local

Schoolhouse #3 on Manchester Road circa 1890. Note that most of the boys are barefoot.

schools were poorly maintained, with holes present in the walls and roof. The school board asked one Derry teacher in 1868 if her schoolhouse was well ventilated. She replied, "Ventilated? On cold days, it is well ventilated!" There was also a significant difference in the school population between districts. In one district in 1868 there were sixty-three students in one school but only three in another. Before 1900, the age of the students within a single classroom could range from three to eighteen.

Many schools before the mid-nineteenth century even lacked the most basic sanitary facilities. Teachers and students were forced to relieve themselves in the bushes that surrounded the schools. As late as 1906, the outhouses were classified by the superintendent as "disgraceful and neither conducive to good health nor a high standard of morality." Drinking water came via a pail brought from a neighboring farmer's well. The students and teachers all drank from the same ladle when they were thirsty.

The nineteenth century's school year was traditionally divided into two terms. A schoolmaster taught the winter term because it was thought that only a man could handle the discipline problems caused by rambunctious boys. A schoolmistress taught the summer term because the boys stayed home to do farm chores. The only qualification to teach was usually a letter of recommendation from a pastor or another teacher. Few of the district schoolteachers had any education beyond the district school itself. Most teachers were simply farmers with free time in the winter or the unmarried daughters of local farmers. The town report would annually note how well each teacher handled his or her class. His or her successes or failures were publically published for everyone to read. The poorer school districts usually employed only the less experienced, less skilled teachers and often had a new teacher every term.

Before the Civil War, many students didn't have textbooks, and those who did were probably using books that had been passed down from their parents. The town did not furnish schoolbooks until the end of the century. In addition, few schools had many instructional devices. In 1868, only two of the ten district schools had a globe, five had wall maps and only three had a clock. The teacher would often have to guess when it was time to have recess or dismiss the school at the end of the day. Some teachers probably made a mark on a windowsill to act as a primitive sundial. Many schools lacked even a chalkboard. This basic piece of equipment was usually just a smooth board that was painted black and nailed to the classroom wall. One Derry teacher complained that blackboards were "as rare as if they came all the way from Russia."

Most people today believe that early schools were "taught to the rule of the hickory stick." In truth, corporal punishment seems to have been rarely used and was frequently criticized when it was. A teacher scolding the child or having the student stand in the corner handled most discipline problems. In 1866, there were only forty-five incidences of corporal punishment in all the Derry schools—and thirty of those beatings came from the same teacher. Nineteenth-century parents seemed to prefer that the teacher "spare the rod." In 1892, a number of parents petitioned the school board to not force their little darlings to walk home in the rain if they were kept after class. Positive reinforcement was highly praised. Children who didn't whisper or come to school tardy would find their names listed in the town report as an example to others.

With the development of the shoe factories in western Derry during the late nineteenth century, there was suddenly the need to create a Broadway school district. A former one-room bank building was made into an elementary school for the older students; a small wooden building was built for the primary children. Soon these buildings were filled to the bursting point. In 1892, for example, the elementary school had 67 students being taught by a single teacher; the primary school had 128 little children taught by one teacher and an aide. In 1895, the board of health closed these schools. This, the school board said, "was something the winter cold and smoke has almost accomplished all by itself."

The town's school board now had no choice but to build new schools for the children of West Derry's shoe workers. The East Side and West Side Schools were both originally two-room, single story buildings. Within a decade of their construction, they also had become overcrowded, and by 1905 the school population had swelled to the point where thirty-nine students were being taught in the basement of the Adams Memorial Building. To add more classrooms and save the expense of replacing the roof, the East Side and West Side Schools were jacked up into the air and new classrooms were constructed underneath. The original first floor thus became the new second floor. These schools were closed in 1952. The West Side School is now the Marion Gerrish Community Center, and the East Side School is currently an apartment building.

Within another decade, the Broadway schools were again overcrowded, and the courtroom was being used as a first-grade classroom. For the first

West Side School (circa 1895) is now a story higher and is home to the Marion Gerrish Community Center on Broadway.

time, the school board required entering students to be at least six years old. To further ease the crowding, the Floyd School on Highland Avenue was built in 1915. The school was named after Charles Floyd, the state's only governor to come from Derry. The school was closed in 2005.

Also in 1915, the first Parent-Teacher Association was formed in Derry, with Jennie Grinnell, the wife of the school superintendent, as its president. Among its first projects was a plan to bring a dental clinic to the schools. In 1929, it led the drive for vocational training at the East Side Junior High School. In 1953, they made a deal with a local dairy farm so all five hundred Derry students could buy a daily bottle of milk for a penny. In 1942, they helped start the first hot lunch program and promoted modern math in 1965.

After World War II, the school population again began to grow as the returning soldiers began to start families. There seemed to be no end in sight to this school enrollment bubble as the number of school kids in Derry doubled. To help solve the problem of overcrowding, three new schools were built between 1952 and 1955: the Grinnell Elementary School, named after Judge Herbert Grinnell; the Gilbert H. Hood Junior High School, donated by Helen Hood in honor of her husband; and the St. Thomas Aquinas Parochial School. These large, modern schools allowed the school board to close the old district schools in East Derry and Derry Village, as well as the East Side and West Side Schools.

The school population continued to grow steadily throughout the 1950s but really began to spike with the opening of Interstate I-93. In 1965, the school population grew 27 percent in a single year! There was now a crisis in the classroom. Desks had to be pushed within a foot of the chalkboard, as classrooms designed to hold thirty students had to service forty or more. Gyms and locker rooms had to do double duty as classrooms. By 1965, the school enrollment had reached about thirteen hundred students.

Because of the school's population explosion, the residents saw their tax bill spike as new schools were built. In 1966, the South Range School was opened. The new Derry Village School was built in 1967, and the old 1901 Derry Village School became the school district office. To save taxpayers some money, the budget committee killed a proposal for a public kindergarten. It would not be until 2008 that taxpayer-supported kindergarten began in Derry, making the town one of the last eleven towns in the state to offer public preschool.

Despite the school building programs of the 1960s, schools continued to be overcrowded as apartment complexes, trailer parks and housing developments sprang up everywhere. Between the years 1967 and 1970, the school population swelled from 1,600 to 2,300 students. The town had to

By the 1990s, most Derry schools had become very overcrowded, as demonstrated by this scene at the Hood Junior High School. *Photo by Jim Pavia*, Derry News.

impose a strict cap on new residential construction to help manage the school population. The superintendent even had to negotiate with a local church to rent classroom space. For three years in a row, the cash-strapped voters turned down building an addition to the Hood School, but finally the crisis was so dramatic that in 1970 they voted 712 to 187 to fund the expansion. The crowding was helped somewhat by the opening of the Calvary Christian School in 1970. With its emphasis on back-to-basics, Bible-centered teaching and dedicated staff, it soon proved a success. At present, there are up to two hundred students enrolled in its classes from kindergarten to grade twelve. In mid-July 2009, the school announced that it would be closing due to the effects of the national economic recession.

In 1997, the state mandated that Derry add new classrooms despite the opening of the new West Running Brook Middle School. The previously closed Floyd School was reopened to ease the overcrowding. The Ernest F. Barka School was opened in 2005 and named after a popular school board member. At present, there are 4,077 students enrolled in the school district, as well as another 2,278 enrolled in high school at Pinkerton Academy.

Other sources of learning in town are the two public libraries. The Taylor Library was opened in February 1878 thanks to a $1,000 bequest from Miss Harriett Taylor. The library during its first forty years was housed in an upper room at the Upper Village Hall. In 1929, Frederick Shepard Jr. provided the funds to build the present neocolonial brick library. The books were moved from the old building to the new by a brigade of patrons including six-year-old future astronaut Alan Shepard. In the first years, library cards were only given to individuals whom the board of examiners thought "suitable."

When West Derry became the population center of the town, many wished to move the Taylor Library to where most of the people lived. Those in East Derry were opposed to this idea. The compromise was to have two libraries. The Derry Public Library was originally established in the Adams Memorial Building with a gift of $1,000 from Rosecrans Pillsbury in 1905. It soon became overcrowded, and in 1927 it was moved to the new McGregor Library building on East Broadway. Henry McGregor had grown up locally but moved to Texas as a young man. As a real estate speculator, he soon became very wealthy. For decades he ran the Texas Republican Party from his real estate office, controlled Houston's trolley system and was instrumental in the building of the Houston Ship Canal. He also left funds to build Pioneer Park next to the library. A large addition was added to the library in 1990.

PINKERTON ACADEMY

The small Classical High School that had been started on East Derry Hill in 1793 had fallen on hard times by 1812. The tuition paid by its twenty students was not sufficient to pay the $120 annual salary of Principal Samuel Burnham. The trustees tried unsuccessfully to spark some life into the school by building a new two-story building on the site of today's Taylor Library. Reverend Edward Parker of the First Parish Church decided to start a new high school—this time with a permanent endowment to make it economically viable during hard times. After many false starts, he finally found support from brothers Major John and Elder James Pinkerton.

The Pinkertons were local merchants who made their fortune by farming, running a pair of stores and loaning money at interest. Major John gave $13,158.18 and Elder James donated $1,500.00. There was considerable squabbling among the trustees as to whether the new school should be located in East Derry or Derry Village. After a protracted lawsuit, Gregg's Hill in Derry Village came out the winner. In 1814, Samuel Burnham, who had been principal of the old Classical High School, was hired as preceptor (principal) of Pinkerton Academy. His annual salary was $200 plus $2 for every student enrolled. Among his responsibilities was to lead the students in prayer and "set the highest moral tone" for the students.

During the first year a small school building was built on top of Gregg's Hill. This building soon proved too small, and a front porch was added and its two classrooms were divided to make four rooms. The enrollment that first year was seventy-one students with about half being from outside the town. Most of the students boarded at private homes in the village, with only nine living at home. Each weekend, the students from Chester walked ten miles to get home, every student carrying a sack of dirty laundry for their mothers to wash. Only one-third of the first students were female, and the youngest student at the academy in 1814 was just eight years old. Throughout the nineteenth century the school's enrollment fell to just twenty-eight students.

In 1881, Boston lawyer John Morrison Pinkerton bequeathed over $200,000 to the academy for a new building. The original academy building was moved a short distance to the west, and the new Pinkerton building erected in its place. This new brick structure was built in the popular Romanesque style and was topped with a 125-foot-tall clock tower with a 1,530-pound bell. In 1884, the school purchased the nearby Sander's Hotel to be used as a boarding hall for its students and renamed it Hildreth Hall.

The original 1814 Pinkerton Academy building (left) and the new Pinkerton building (right) built in 1885. Photo circa 1905.

Art class at Pinkerton Academy, 1895.

Pinkerton Academy during the nineteenth century should not be confused with a modern high school. It was, instead, a private preparatory school in the same mode as Philips Exeter Academy. It was not supported by public taxes nor did the town pay the tuition of any local students. It was, in fact, a school for the sons and daughters of the elite. In 1877, a local judge wrote an article in the *Exeter News-Letter* in opposition to Derry building its own high school. In his mind, such a project wouldn't be viable because Derry would *never* have more than fifty students at one time with sufficient ability to enter a high school.

During the administration of Headmaster George Bingham (1885–1909), there was a culture war going on in Derry. A growing number of locals believed that a high school education would benefit the children of shoe factory workers and farmers. This equalitarian idea was successfully fought off by Bingham and most of the board of trustees who wanted the curriculum to remain heavy with instruction in Latin, Greek and classical literature. In 1892, the town meeting voted against offering any scholarships for academy students. In addition to the cost, another barrier to entering Pinkerton was the admission test. In 1905, only three Derry students successfully passed this exam on the first try. Many potential students got discouraged and did not try for a retake. Most children only finished the eighth grade.

Under Headmaster Ernest Silver (1909–11) things began to change. While some aspects of the classical curriculum were retained, much was added. Among the radical course changes were instruction in home economics, typing and farming. To get around the dreaded admissions test, the public school superintendent was allowed to certify that certain eighth-grade students were sufficiently prepared for the rigors of high school. The town also began to pay the tuition of the students who wanted a secondary education. Despite these changes, however, it still wouldn't be until after World War II that most local students received a high school diploma.

Before the construction of I-93, the academy's enrollment never exceeded 400 students. In 1976, its student count passed 1,000 for the first time, and the school was forced to erect "temporary" portable classrooms that still are being used today. The enrollment at present is 3,300 students, making Pinkerton Academy the largest private academy in the nation and one that occupies a multi-acre campus with fifteen major buildings. Its alumni and teachers have included poet Robert Frost, astronaut Alan Shepard Jr., newspaper editor/politician Robert Lincoln O'Brian, television personality Samantha Brown and Olympian Trish Dunn. To date Pinkerton remains a private school, but most of its funding comes from public sources.

ADAMS FEMALE ACADEMY

When Pinkerton Academy opened in 1814, a third of its students were female. Suddenly, without explanation, in 1824 the trustees decided to make Pinkerton Academy an all-male school. About this time, local farmer Jacob Adams left a bequest of $3,650 to start a girls' school. That year the Adams Female Academy opened in the former Classical High School on East Derry Hill. In 1829, this two-story, twenty-eight- by forty-foot building was moved to a lot on nearby Lane Road. Soon the trustees built a three-story boardinghouse to serve as a dormitory for both teachers and students.

The first preceptress (principal) was Miss Zilpah Polly Grant, who would later become a leader in the feminist movement. Her assistant was Miss Mary Lyon, who would later go on to found Mount Holyoke College—America's first women's college. Room and board at the Adams school was $1.50 per week and tuition was $6.00 for a fourteen-week-long term. The school was closed from December to March, as the winter climate in Derry was not "favorable." The first year there were 71 students enrolled at the school; the number jumped to 116 as the reputation of the school began to spread.

The Adams Female Academy was considered to be the nation's first endowed girls' school that issued diplomas, had a published curriculum and owned its own building. The school prided itself in that it taught the girls the same way that boys were taught in college. Among its trustees and on its board of examiners were future president Franklin Pierce, U.S. senator Samuel Bell, Governor John Bell and essayist Ralph Waldo Emerson. In 1825, General Lafayette visited the school to see where "females are treated as rational beings." Included in its curriculum were courses in algebra, orthography, economics, chemistry, philosophy, logic and modern and ancient languages. The school's demand for excellence is reflected in its motto "Drink deep or taste not," which had been written by poet Alexander Pope. For many months, Miss Grant had to teach lying down because she had injured herself doing calisthenics with her girls.

In 1826, the relations between the trustees and Misses Grant and Lyon began to deteriorate over the school's mission. These ladies were very public in their belief that teaching was a holy mission for which they would be held accountable on the Day of Judgment. At the start of each term, the ladies divided their students into two categories—saved and unsaved. There were daily Bible readings, and it was said that at the Adams Female Academy the students read more scripture than at any school except for theological institutions. Lyon and Grant took part in several local revival meetings and openly "prayed for the influence of the Holy Spirit" on the school.

The Adams Female Academy, Lane Road, East Derry, 1900.

The trustees demanded less proselytizing, less scripture reading and the introduction of classes in dancing. Grant and Lyon refused, saying that such changes would disrupt the "systematically" taught curriculum and introducing dancing would be "evil." While the trustees were willing to compromise, Grant and Lyon would not. On January 7, 1828, the two ladies resigned and left the school, taking with them forty of the students.

The school never fully recovered from the loss of Lyon and Grant, and its enrollment began to decline. In 1853, Pinkerton Academy began to readmit girls as students, and the enrollment at the Adams school went down even more. In addition, the Adams Female Academy was no longer the nation's only high-quality girls' school. There were now many excellent girls' schools scattered across America; former students of Misses Grant and Lyon, in fact, started many of these. The school limped along until 1886, when it was sold to the town and used as a district school. The building was sold in 1953 and is now a private residence. The funds from the sale of the school are used today to provide scholarships for local students.

CHAPTER 4

FIRE PROTECTION

Prior to 1828, Derry had no official fire protection. The only possible way to extinguish a fire was the bucket brigade. Dozens of men, women and children would form a line to pass pails of water from a stream or well. A second line would be formed to bring the pail back for a refill. The church bell would be rung to bring reinforcements to the scene. Usually, however, such efforts proved ineffective, and the best that could be hoped was that the fire didn't spread.

The town meeting in 1828 appointed five men as fire wards but did not appoint anyone to buy any firefighting equipment. It did buy a six-foot-long red-painted pole with a brass finial. This was called the "badge of office." Whoever held the pole at a fire was the person in command. Failure to follow his orders could result in a fifty-dollar fine—a huge sum in those days. An eighteen-man fire department was established in 1831. When a fire call came in, they were expected to drop whatever they were doing and run to the fire. They were paid for their services and fined a dollar if they ignored the call. Derry's first fire engine was a tiny Hunneman-type pumper that measured about six feet in length. For the next fifty years, there seemed to be no more financial support for fire protection in Derry.

On Saturday, August 19, 1882, a fire broke out in a stable of Derry's Railroad Hotel. Quickly the tongues of fire spread throughout the entire depot area. Within minutes the hotel was gone, followed by Hood's icehouse, the depot and the freight station. This fire soon destroyed the Pillsbury block, the Baptist meeting hall and the railroad company's fuel storage shed that contained three hundred cords of wood. The barbershop, post office and ice cream parlor were soon smoldering ruins. The heat became so intense that it buckled the railroad tracks, twisting them into strange shapes pointed skyward. The Great Fire of 1882 destroyed altogether twenty-four buildings or businesses. It was only because of the swift arrival of a Manchester fire engine that prevented the whole downtown from being lost.

While the fire was still smoldering, it was decided that the town needed a fire department. The fire had almost destroyed the shoe factory that was perceived as the key to Derry's future success. The next town meeting voted to spend $3,000 to establish three separate but unequal fire departments. West Derry got $1,500; Derry Village received $900; and East Derry, $600. This formula was likely based on the population of the three villages. Added to this equation was the fact that West Derry had many factories and stores, Derry Village has a slightly smaller population with a few stores and a couple of factories and East Derry had the smallest population with a commercial base consisting of a single country store.

West Derry and Derry Village each purchased a hand-pumped fire engine. Men attached by leather harnesses like horses pulled these engines to fires. Once in place, teams of men would fill its reservoir with bucketfuls of water; other teams of brawny men would pump up and down on the engine's lever to force water through a canvas hose held by a third team of firemen. When things worked perfectly, with the three teams coordinating their efforts, the engines could pump a jet of water higher than the steeple of the Baptist church.

Each fireman was to be paid three dollars per year and thirty cents per hour while actually fighting fires. West Derry and Derry Village each built a small garage to hold their fire engine. It is not known how East Derry spent its money, but there is no evidence that it bought a fire engine; possibly fire hooks or a chemical extinguisher were purchased. This meant that East Derry remained without any fire protection, because it would be impossible for teams of men to pull a heavy fire engine up East Derry Hill.

Derry was now officially divided into three fire districts. If you lived within a half mile of Broadway, Pinkerton Academy or the Upper Village Hall then you were in a fire district. Most of the town was outside any of the three fire districts. If you lived within a district you were taxed for fire protection. If you lived outside a fire district, you paid no fire district tax. Only those within a district would be guaranteed fire protection. If you lived outside a district, a fire engine might or might not be sent to quell your fire. Even if the district fire chief did agree to send his engine outside his district, it could take an hour or more to get to the blaze. Oftentimes by the time the engine arrived, it would be too late, and all there was left was a smoking cellar hole. Regardless of whether the engine arrived in a timely manner or not, you would still be sent a bill for $100.

The Derry Depot Fire Department in 1899 built a modern brick fire station on West Broadway. In its basement were stabled two horses always ready to pull their new steam-powered pumper to a fire. Its location was significant as it was only about fifty feet from the Pillsbury Shoe Factory. A few years later, the Derry Village Fire Department built a two-story engine house on Crescent Street. In 1909, the Derry Depot Fire Department officially changed its name to the Derry Fire Department.

In 1914–15, three massive fires shook West Derry: in March, the Adams Memorial Building containing the town offices and library was destroyed; in August, flames leveled the Catholic church; and during the next year, the Woodbury Shoe Factory was totally destroyed in a fire that left hundreds out of work. The voters of the district were now convinced that it was time to bring the fire department into modern times. The old horse-drawn steam pumper was replaced by the largest, most modern piece of fire equipment in the state—a new American-LaFrance six-cylinder, self-propelled combination pumper, tanker, chemical engine and hose truck. It was powered by a one-hundred-horsepower engine and could pump eight hundred gallons of water per minute. This nine-thousand-pound fire truck could speed to fires at sixty miles per hour carrying 1,200 feet of fire hose. The district also purchased a mechanical respirator machine to treat those suffering from smoke inhalation. Frank Hurd, the town's first full-

The new American-LaFrance fire engine goes for a demonstration ride in 1915.

time fireman, was hired in 1915 at fifteen dollars per week; he was on duty twenty-four hours per day, seven days per week.

In 1920, Derry Village decided to hire the Derry Fire District (DFD) for protection. With their new American-LaFrance truck, they could be in the village within minutes. That year there was also a gathering of fifty men in East Derry to discuss if their nonfunctioning fire district should buy any fire equipment. It was voted instead to hire the DFD to protect the immediate area around the First Parish Church. Despite these votes, most of the town remained outside of any district, and it was well known that the DFD fire chief would frequently refuse to send his big new fire truck to the rural areas of the town.

After a number of destructive fires, it was decided in 1928 to form an effective fire department in East Derry. It was incorporated in 1932 as a private non-town-owned fire department, with Ned Reynolds as chief. Originally, its retrofitted Model T fire truck was housed in a barn, but in 1934 the town allowed a garage bay to be cut into the Upper Village Hall. In 1936, the East Derry Fire Department had acquired considerable debt with no way to pay it off. It was voted that the residents of East Derry would buy the department for one dollar and created the publicly funded East Derry Fire District (EDFD). It wouldn't be until 1948 that the EDFD bought its first factory-built fire engine. Its first full-time fireman was hired in 1970 when it moved into a modern fire station.

In 1959, the selectmen decided that the whole town should have fire protection. The town was then divided between DFD and EDFD. The taxpayers were taxed to support the fire district in which they lived. By this time, many in town began to debate if it would be more effective to merge the two districts to avoid a duplication of services. There was a difference between the two districts. The DFD used mainly full-time firemen; the EDFD with a smaller number of full-time professional firemen relied on a larger percentage of highly motivated "call firemen who worked full time in other jobs but responded when a fire call came in." The DFD, starting in 1970, operated the town's ambulance and in 1979 hired Donald Gelinas as its first certified paramedic. In 1964, the DFD built the modern central fire station in Derry Village.

To fully report on the battle of the merging of the two fire districts would require hundreds of pages. The constraints of space forces the story to be retold in relatively few paragraphs. This narration is a mere summary of events that occurred over a span of thirty years and involved hundreds of people. The passion and red-faced anger of Derry residents on both sides of the issue can only be imperfectly reported here.

Aerial shot of Chelmsford Shoe Factory fire of 1960. *Courtesy of David A. MacGregor Jr.*

While merger talks began in the 1960s, it would not be until 1973 that the discussions got serious. That year a vote was taken on having a single fire district. To achieve this merge, it would take a two-thirds vote of both fire districts. The DFD was reputably OK with a merger if the EDFD would first agree to dissolve. In East Derry, the vote was "yes" by an overwhelming majority of 109 to 55. The motion failed, however, because it missed being a two-thirds majority by just one vote.

Despite the highly charged debate by the voters, the two fire departments routinely cooperated. A mutual aid agreement was formalized in 1976. There were occasional problems, however, such as in 1978 when the two chiefs got into a public tiff. The DFD had responded to an automobile accident on Route 102. Its Jaws of Life™ was used to free the driver, who was hanging by his leg upside down in his car. The accident was inside the EDFD, and Chief Arthur Reynolds was reported in the newspaper as being upset that DFD chief James Cote did not have "the common decency" to notify his office when coming into his district.

In 1986, the EDFD asked the town to give it a four-acre piece of land near Bypass 28 on which to build a sub-station. The council refused, saying that the location was inappropriate for a fire station. Many in the EDFD took this decision hard, viewing it as interference on the sovereignty of the EDFD and a suggestion, by inference, that they could not run a fire department. Many years later, the EDFD would acquire some land and built a sub-station on Bypass 28 without council involvement.

For the next fourteen years, the efforts to unite the two districts never moved beyond the debating stage. It was thought by many as being an idea that would probably never happen—like the United States going fully metric or the British driving on the right-hand side of the road. The debate became red hot when on September 19, 2000, the town council voted 4 to 2 to redraw the boundary line of the DFD. A petition of some East Derry residents requesting a redesign of the boundaries brought about this move. A consulting firm hired by the council had issued a report that the public would be better served if the DFD took over half the land within the EDFD.

The immediate effect of this boundary shift was to rob from the EDFD about 52 percent of its tax base. If remaining taxpayers in East Derry Fire District wanted to continue having their own fire department, they would now have to pony up a lot more in taxes. The boundary shift also meant that one of EDFD's commissioners and its clerk no longer lived in the district and that the new EDFD sub-station now belonged to the DFD. The boundary change was quickly challenged in court.

The Superior Court in August 2003 ruled that the boundary change was "capricious and arbitrary." The court ordered the council to develop "reasonable boundaries" and hold public hearings. A daylong hearing was held in November, and the council voted a "modicum of a modification" to the 2000 boundaries. In East Derry, a fire district meeting resulted in a 150 to 40 vote to reject the November concession and expressed the desire to return to the "historic" pre-2000 boundary.

After receiving word of the rejection by the EDFD, the town council on April 1, 2004, voted to go back again to the 2000 boundary. It also voted to close the Bypass 28 sub-station. The EDFD taxpayers now saw a doubling of their tax bill for fire protection. Demonstrators now began to appear at council meetings protesting the boundary change.

An emergency appeal was sent to the Superior Court on April 2, 2004. This time the court sided with the town council. Judge Tina Nadeau ruled that the East Derry residents were adequately protected by the September 19, 2000 boundary. In May the court rejected another appeal. The EDFD commissioners decided to continue the legal battle despite losing twice in court and having legal expenses over $200,000. Later in 2004 the Derry Firemen's Union, the Officer's Union and the East Derry Firefighter's Union voted 51 to 9 to merge into a single union.

In the wake of the court's ruling, the EDFD began to look for ways to cut expenses. In October 2004, it began to lay off firemen, with each shift having two less firemen. The laid-off firemen were immediately hired by the DFD. In November 2004, EDFD chief John Nadeau was asked for his resignation and given a severance package of $88,577.21. This golden parachute was ruled illegal in November 2005. Nadeau and Commissioner Lundblad have agreed to repay most of money to the town.

By the fall of 2004, most residents of the town just wanted the fighting between the DFD and EDFD to go away. Each side was spending hundreds of thousands of dollars on lawyers and court fees. People in East Derry could expect their tax bills to rise by perhaps $600. In November, the courts ruled once more against the EDFD. Undaunted by this ruling, the commissioners said that they would continue to fight in court. Derry Council chairman Jim MacEachern expressed disappointment that the EDFD wouldn't "end it and move on." In December, the East Derry firemen voted that the two departments should merge.

During all this commotion, things were not going well inside the EDFD's governing board. Several commissioners resigned, and charges were publicly aired about illegal appointments; secret, closed-door meetings; and violations of the Right to Know laws. Commissioner David McPherson was threatening to sue commissioners June Fahey and Allan Lundblad for making decisions at meetings of which he had not been notified. In turn, Fahey and Lundblad were threatening to sue McPherson for illegally releasing information from nonpublic commission meetings.

In December, Fahey and Lundblad resigned, leaving David McPherson as the sole remaining commissioner. He appointed Paul Dionne to the commission, and together they appointed David Milz as the third commissioner. The three men voted to cease all pending lawsuits. The battle was over. At the March 2005 EDFD election, pro-merger candidates easily defeated those who wanted to keep the two districts separate. The will of the people was to end the fight. Derry was to have a single fire district. On December 31, 2005, the books of the East Derry Fire District were closed after seventy-seven years of dedicated service.

CHAPTER 5

LAW AND ORDER

The first law enforcement agent in old Nutfield was Justice John McKeen (1665–1756), who was appointed magistrate in 1720. He would in effect be our first district court judge and would try minor civil offences. More serious cases would be sent to the royal court in Portsmouth. Regretfully, no records survived from McKeen's court. The town clerk's records do mention a few trials such as the 1730 case of Lieutenant Hugh Wilson, who was "prosecuted as an idler." In 1739, the selectmen ordered Daniel Macpherson locked in handcuffs and leg irons to prevent him from "hurting or disturbing" others. The town refused to pay anything for his room and board; instead, he would be passed from home to home with everyone in town keeping him for twenty-four hours. There was a fine of ten shillings for refusing to take a turn in caring for Macpherson.

Most references to early law enforcement come from the records of the local Presbyterian Society. The church ran its own court system to enforce the moral standards of the community. Among the people and charges brought before the pastor and elders included: James Doaks, for hitting his father (1726); Thomas Smith, for selling liquor to Indians (1727); William Eyars and widow Mary Campbell, for lying in bed together naked; Miss Marion Gleen, for not seeking help during the birth of her child when help would have saved the infant's life (1731); and William Magoo, for profanity (1733). The guilty were made to admit the "sins" before the congregation or to be excommunicated from the fellowship.

The known first "real" crime occurred in 1770 when during a quarrel Robert Dickey killed Robert Moore with an axe. He was acquitted in Portsmouth because Dickey "had no intension or design to kill Moore." It appears that the crime rate did accelerate in the nineteenth century, because in 1828 Derry constructed its own "house of correction." The punishable crimes included being "a rogue, vagabond, lewd or disorderly person…going about juggling or begging or persons using subtle crafts, unlawful games or plays…common night walkers…and those who misspend what they earn." The punishment for those "crimes" was to spend ninety days shackled with chains in a dark cell or being made to work at hard labor. The prisoners were given only the traditional "bread and water" diet.

During the remainder of the century, the town passed a few laws and other ordinances, which probably reflected what was going on in Derry. In 1840, they passed an ordinance against "indecent swimming or bathing." The police regulations in 1885 forbade "seats for loafers" in front of stores on Sundays, smoking in stables, loud noise at night and "stamping, whistling, or making other disturbances at the town hall." Pool halls and saloons had to close at 10:00 p.m. and could not open on Sundays at all.

Derry did have a local court from 1833 to 1866, but its first police court did not open until 1895. Its first judge was William W. Poor, who had no legal training and likely lacked even a high school diploma. He received $100 per year for sitting on the bench, where he presided over trials that involved public intoxications, brawling, petty thefts and juvenile delinquency.

When the railroad first came to Derry in 1849, it carried with it great economic and social benefits; there were, however, a few problems brought in as well. Tramps riding in boxcars would frequently stop over in Derry. Some would go door to door begging for food or money; a few would offer to work for their supper; and still others would steal whatever was left out in plain sight. Whenever the local police found one of these "transient fellows," he would be hauled off to a local hotel for the night. In the morning, the hobo would be fed a basic breakfast and put on the next train out of town. In 1901, the Hotel Bradford gave room and board to fifty-eight tramps at a total cost to the taxpayer of $20.30. Other groups given the "bums rush" out of town were caravans of gypsies, handicapped beggars and backpack peddlers. They were all prejudged to be guilty of potentially causing some breach of public order and were thus kicked out before they could do harm.

Gambling was very common in Derry during the past centuries. One-armed bandits were openly displayed in stores, bars and social clubs. While they were illegal, storekeepers skirted the law by having them only pay out tokens good for mint candies. In truth, these tokens could be redeemed for cash if the counterman knew the winner. With one machine at the Beaver Lake Pavilion, a patron could win twenty-five cigars for a nickel bet. The "large cash machine" had a two-dollar payout that was equal to a day's wages for the average shoe factory worker. In 1904, it was reported that on Broadway there were ten-year-old boys playing the "fruit machines."

One raid by federal authorities in 1913 yielded twenty gambling machines in Derry.

Gambling continued to be a local problem right up to the present day. In 2001, the federal authorities began to investigate complaints from women that their husbands were spending much of their paycheck on video poker machines. These machines were labeled as being "for amusement only," but winning points could be exchanged for cash. In September 2004, the police raided the Eagles and Halcyon Clubs, where nine poker machines and over $13,000 were confiscated.

In 1964, New Hampshire decided to be the first in the nation to have a sweepstakes. Tickets could only be purchased at state liquor stores. The winner was to be determined by a horserace at Salem's Rockingham Park. Locally, the first ticket was sold on March 24 to Representative Charles "Cap" Gay. The proceeds, then and now, help fund education. The first year, Derry's share was $24,944.78, which was about equal to the yearly salary of five classroom teachers.

From the earliest days of the town, the local authorities have tried to restrict the sale of wine, beer, hard cider or spirits. Taverns and stores that sold liquor were required to have licenses that had to be renewed annually. The idea that drinking was immoral began in the local churches about 1834. The temperance movement would try for the next century to forbid the sale of alcohol in town. For some years, Derry was officially dry, and all bars were ordered closed; during other years, the town was wide open, and Broadway was very wet. In 1827, Derry had five taverns and seven stores that sold alcoholic drinks by the glassful. The town's population was then about 2,100 people. This translates into one drinking establishment for every 175 people or about one bar for every 50 men. We really did seem to be a "right, tight little town" in those days.

During 1855–60, the town would not issue any liquor licenses and instead started selling alcohol itself. Storekeeper Charles Parker was appointed liquor agent and was allowed to sell alcohol only for "medicinal and mechanical purposes and wine to commemorate the Lord's Supper and no other purpose whatever." That year Parker sold eighty-three gallons of rum, twenty-nine gallons of brandy, four and a half gallons of wine, twenty-one gallons of gin and one bottle of port wine. The town made a profit of 10 percent on all these liquor sales.

The Women's Christian Temperance League of Derry was founded in 1883 and led the local drive toward prohibition. The men of the Law and Order League joined them in 1895. The league spent much of its time sending out spies to ferret out illegal liquor sellers. Upon discovery of such

A West Derry barroom on Central Street in 1905.

an establishment, the league members would blockade the doors of the place and not let anyone in or out. The police would be called and another bar bit the dust.

During World War I, the town went dry with a wartime prohibition; after the war, the Eighteenth Amendment went into effect. Alcohol now became the forbidden fruit and seemingly more attractive by being kind of "naughty and slightly illegal." Soon the local newspapers were filled with tales of federal agents raiding homes where "bath tub" gin was being manufactured or finding stills in the woods of the Seven Hills region of West Derry. In 1923, the local police were engaged in a high-speed chase up Ryan's Hill pursuing bootleggers. As the rumrunners sped toward Salem in their huge Hupmobile sedan, they were firing guns at the police while throwing cans of hooch out the car's windows.

Prohibition never seemed to be very popular in the working-class town of Derry. On June 20, 1933, a special election was held in the state on the repeal of Prohibition. In Derry the citizens voted 807 to 471 to bring back their beer and gin fizzes. After the tally was announced at 7:00 p.m., a crowd began to gather at Keith's Lunch Room on Maple Street. It was decided that the glorious occasion called for a parade. Two buglers and a man with a bass drum led the marchers down the street while everyone belted out endless choruses of "Happy Days Are Here Again." Following behind was a small army of men wearing "flowered ladies hats from days gone-by." They were soon joined by "high heeled farmeretts" and others carrying signs proclaiming "Am I Happy!" A thousand spectators let out a cheer as the parade snaked down Broadway. At the end of the line rolled a slow-moving truck. Its back was filled with kegs of beer from which Red Lambert and his friends were pouring mugs of beer to everyone who felt thirsty. This was their first legal drink in sixteen years.

In the early twentieth century, the town's police force was a very small operation. The first police chief was Albert Roberts, who in 1903 had a force of just three part-time patrolmen. When they were off duty, there was no thin blue line protecting the town. In 1934, the selectmen finally decided to institute round-the-clock police protection. One officer would be on duty from 6:00 a.m. to 6:00 p.m., and then he would be relieved for the night by the police chief. Every two weeks, they alternated shifts. Each week they were given two days off when a third officer would fill in. Thirty "special" policemen who could be called in during emergencies reinforced this tiny police force.

The police station in 1910 was the basement of the Adams Memorial Town Hall. Toward the back were three jail cells—each measured about six feet square and was made of flat strap steel. An indoor shooting range was also located in the station. Here officers could fire their weapons down range about thirty feet into a sand-filled target. Directly above the target was a piece of thick steel that was raised into place during shooting to prevent ricochets from going into the ceiling. One day an officer forgot to put this barrier in place, and a bullet went through the ceiling, just missing a selectman sitting in his first-floor office. After that incident the firing range was permanently moved outside. Oftentimes citizens would call the police station, but the officer would be walking his Broadway beat. To facilitate a ready response, a blue light would flash on the outside of the building to let the patrolman know that there was a call. He would then have to run back to the station or pick up an extension at the Odd Fellows Block.

Over the years, the Adams Building Police Station had grown rather shabby and overcrowded. In 1971, Judge George Grinnell called the lockup "deplorable." There was no parking, little ventilation and a total lack of privacy, plus it was infested with mice and the jerry-rigged electrical systems made it a firetrap. In 1982, ground was broken for a new $1.5 million modern station at the site of the old Ross Dairy Farm at Ross's Corner. Local businessman Steven Grover donated much of the land.

In 1972, the selectmen ruled that age sixty-five was the mandatory retirement age for all police officers, forcing Chief Kenneth Bisbee to turn in his badge. In his place the town hired Lebanon, New Hampshire police captain Edward Garone. In the past, chiefs were locals who learned their craft on the job. The twenty-nine-year-old Garone was the town's first police chief with college course work in law enforcement. His pay that year was $14,000, which was nearly $4,000 more than his predecessor. Among his first acts as chief was the crackdown of drug dealing and backyard pot gardens. Now after thirty-seven years on the job, Ed Garone is still chief and shows no signs of retiring.

There have been three major crimes during the last forty years that have put Derry on the map. The first centered on the criminal exploits of Mark McDermott. He moved to town in 1967 and the next year paid off a welfare debt plowing snow for the town. By 1970, he became Derry's first water and sewer commissioner. He apparently was never appointed to the office; instead he just kind of moved into the office, and no one questioned his right to run the department. In 1975, the selectmen discovered that he had stolen $142,000 of public money. Mark made a run for it and was on the lam for over two years. After finally being apprehended, he was sentenced to two and a half to five years in prison. He was paroled after serving only one year of his sentence. Derry got back only $40,000 of its missing money.

McDermott quickly violated the terms of his parole and disappeared. In time, he was discovered in Cuba, where he had spent two years in jail for smuggling drugs. Through the efforts of Reverend Jesse Jackson, he was finally released to the American authorities in 1984. He was immediately rearrested on charges of stealing a car back in 1977. While in prison awaiting trial, he confessed to murdering a Meredith, New Hampshire man. This confession was later thrown out by the Superior Court—his Miranda warning had not been given to him as a part of this confession. After being held for three years in prison without trial, he was ordered released in 1989. His present location is unknown.

On the evening of May 1, 1990, a single shot from a .38-caliber revolver ended the life of twenty-four-year-old Gregory Smart of 4E Misty Morning Drive in Derry. His wife, Pamela Smart, discovered his body. At first, everyone was sympathetic to the grieving widow. In a few months, thanks to excellent detective work by the state and Derry police, the murderer was discovered to be Billy Flynn, who attended school where Mrs. Smart worked. It turned out that Billy was not just her student; he was also her lover. The police were now beginning to theorize that Pam had orchestrated the murder to avoid going through a divorce.

Three months later, Derry detective Daniel R. Pelletier approached Pam in her school's parking lot. He told her, "Well Pam, I have some good news and some bad news. The good news is that we've solved the murder of your

Pamela Smart being led from the court in 1990. Derry News *photo.*

husband. And the bad news is that you're under arrest." After a nationally broadcasted trial, Pam was sentenced to life in prison without the possibility of parole. There have since been two books, two network TV specials and two major Hollywood movies based on the murder.

John "Jay" Brooks had been a local success story. He was a poor boy who grew up with an abusive alcoholic father. He overcame these adversities to become the founder of the Poly Vac Company. He lived in a huge house on Beaver Lake and had a fortune estimated to exceed $100 million. In 2005, he was arrested for the murder of local trucker Jack Reed. It was charged by the police that Brooks had arranged the truck driver's murder because he thought that Reed had stolen a number of items. The missing items included a prized motorcycle and the cremated remains of Jay's father. The trial received national attention because Brooks could have been the first man in sixty years to be sentenced to death in New Hampshire. Despite an experienced and expensive defense team, Brooks was found guilty on November 6, 2008, and sentenced to life imprisonment without the possibility of parole.

CHAPTER 6

TRANSPORTATION

W hen the Ulster Scots arrived in 1719 there were no roads in Nutfield. Perhaps there were a few paths cut through the woods by animals or Indians, but that was all. The first road was laid out in 1721. It ran from the meetinghouse on East Derry Hill to Gregg's Grist and Lumber Mill in Derry Village. It was laid out as two rods wide (thirty-three feet). Other early roads included Broadway (1737), Chester Road (1723) and the road to the Amoskeag Falls (1724). These roads were nothing like those in more modern times; they were unpaved, very narrow and usually lacked culverts or bridges. Often when a road came to a small stream, it would continue through the water. Such fording of streams gave the street, Fordway, its name.

These roads were very rough and rocky. In the spring, they were often no better than miry bogs. For two centuries, the farmers of Derry Village used to supplement their income by pulling vehicles out of the mudholes near today's Danforth traffic circle. Much of the foot traffic, however, was not along the official roads. Cutting through your neighbor's barnyard, wood lot or pasture was not considered trespassing. During the eighteenth century, it is said that East Derry Hill was crisscrossed with a warren of paths that led there from all over the town. They had been blazed by a generation of locals seeking a shortcut to the meetinghouse.

The early residents were great walkers. There are many recorded stories of locals walking to Boston to sell linen thread. Girls in bare feet would hike miles to Sunday meeting and only put on their fancy shoes when arriving at church. A twenty-five-mile hike by an elderly woman was remarkable but not that rare. One woman got lonely for her old neighborhood, so she carried her baby on foot all the way from Vermont to Derry.

During the winter, the isolated farmhouses would often remain snowbound for weeks. From December through March, sleighs and pungs were the

The eastern shore of Beaver Lake about 1895.

standard mode of travel. Local businessman William Pillsbury kept a tally of his travels over a span of fifty years. One year there was sufficient snow cover so he was able to use his sleighs on 126 days. On another year there were only 8 days when sleighing was possible. As late as 1927, farmers were asking that the town's plow trucks leave a little snow on the road so they could use their sleighs.

Early Derry did not have many horses because most farmers preferred oxen for farm work; those who did have horses used the beasts like modern minivans. Going to church a horse could carry a man with his wife on the pillion behind him and with a baby in her arms. It wouldn't be until after the Revolutionary War that a first local man owned a two-wheeled one-horse chaise. It had been purchased by John Prentice, the town's first lawyer, and was considered an "unjustified extravagance." The first mention of a horse-drawn wagon in Derry was in 1814.

The first major highway in town was the Londonderry Turnpike. While other roads were twisty, rutted and filled with rocks and mudholes, the Londonderry Turnpike was straight, smooth and dry. A syndicate of private investors incorporated the highway in 1804 as a for-profit venture running between Methuen, Massachusetts, and Concord, New Hampshire. It was to be four rods wide (sixty-six feet) and to follow the "shortest distances" between

The snow roller as photographed on Highland Avenue about 1910 was used to compact snow on roads to make winter travel easier for sleighs.

the two cities. It is said that huge bonfires were built on hilltops to help the construction workers stay on course. Today the highway, now renamed Route 28 and 28 Bypass, is easy to spot on a map. It is the straightest road in town.

Along the thirty-five-mile-long route, there were six tollgates. At each, a man on horseback was to pay a penny to the gatekeeper; a farmer walking with ten cows was charged two cents. There was no charge for travelers going to church, funerals or for doing business within the town. People who tried sneaking past the tollgate without paying could be made to pay a fine equal to triple the usual rate.

The Londonderry Turnpike was opened in 1806, and soon Derry Village became the economic center of the town. Each day there were dozens of wagons, coaches, carriages and barges rambling down the turnpike. Each night travelers and teamsters were spending the night in the inns in the area. Several doctors and lawyers hung their shingles in the village. Pinkerton Academy, several stores, two churches, a gristmill, an axe factory, a hat manufacturer and rows of stately federal-style homes transformed the area into a true village. The road, however, failed to return the promised profits to its investors and was given to the town in 1831.

The next big transportation development in Derry was the 1847 incorporation of the Manchester and Lawrence Railroad. Both cities were in the forefront of the Industrial Revolution. James Thom of East Derry

The Derry Bicycle Club is shown about 1895 in front of Couch's store in Derry Village. *Courtesy of the Loffler family.*

first proposed the line at a Derry meeting on February 28, 1846. Local legend says that the route was supposed to pass through Derry Village, but its residents vetoed the idea, saying that they did not want a smelly steam locomotive passing through their gentile village. They suggested putting it through the sparsely populated western part of Derry. After the route was finally surveyed, hundreds of Irish laborers began to excavate the rail bed. All went well from Manchester to Derry, but things slowed to a crawl as it passed into Windham. There, a long causeway bridged long stretches of marsh, and a thirteen-foot-deep cut was blasted through ledges.

It would not be until November 13, 1849, that the first train finally traveled through Derry. Freight service began on New Year's Day. Western Derry was soon to have its own post office with the official name of Derry Depot. At this station there was a huge woodshed that held up to three hundred cords of wood to power the steam trains. On the north side of Broadway was a large water tank and a freight office. The rail line would be taken over by the Boston and Maine Corporation in 1887.

Another rail line bisected Derry when the Nashua and Rochester Railroad Company came through the southern part of town in 1874. Its depot was at the foot of Warner Hill and was named Hubbard's Station after Joshua Hubbard, who had owned the property. His deed required that he or his

The railroad causeway that was built in 1849 to create Horne and Hood Pond. *Photo by Leon Rand, 1905.*

The Broadway Railroad Depot in 1904. In the background can be seen the Derry Shoe Factory. *Photo by Leon Rand.*

heirs will "always be the station agent." Its major shipping customer was the Gould Company, which manufactured witch hazel.

Derry received great economic and social benefits from the dozens of trains that were speeding through the town every day. A passenger could board a train on Broadway and arrive in Boston in one hour and eight minutes. A letter could be sent to Massachusetts and an answer received the same day. In August 1896, locals could escape the summer's heat for a $1.50 round-trip ticket to Old Orchard Beach. The big city newspapers were now available every morning at the corner store. Fast freight trains lowered the prices at local stores and greatly added to the variety of items sold in the stores on Broadway. Traveling vaudeville shows now began to pay visits to Derry. Individuals could also visit Boston or Manchester to see Buffalo Bill's Wild West Show or hear Billy Sunday preach.

During the early years of the twentieth century, the railroad was a major factor in the Broadway's industrial prosperity. By 1900, millions of pairs of Derry-made shoes were being shipped by rail each year. The H.P. Hood Company filled several boxcars with their dairy products every day. Every year thousands of gallons of Richardson's boiled vinegar was loaded onto cars at the Broadway freight station. The Derry Mattress Company shipped countless numbers of their product to stores and homes across America. Their slogan was "You'll never awake 'till the crowing of the cock."

There was, however, a downside to having the town cut by train tracks. Each year burning embers from the smokestack of steam trains set small fires in the area. There were also occurrences of speeding trains being involved in deadly accidents. Broadway had a crossing guard who would lower a gate to stop all pedestrian and vehicular traffic whenever a train passed through. The other five crossings in Derry were ungated and were the scene of many tragedies. In 1901, a local had his legs cut off by a Hood boxcar. In 1902, a woman driving a wagon on South Avenue had her horse hit by a train that was speeding through town at sixty miles per hour. Pieces of the poor animal were scattered far up the tracks.

In 1913, locals were horrified to find pieces of Henry Short strewn along the entire length of track from South Avenue to Broadway. In 1921, Roland Rocheleau was driving his automobile on South Avenue when the Boston train hit him. His car was thrown one hundred feet, killing the driver, his fifteen-year-old son and infant daughter. In 1947, Walter Potter's car was hit while crossing North High Street, killing Mr. Porter, his fourteen-year-old son and ten-year-old daughter. The Boston and Maine Corporation had been asked by the town on several occasions to install gates at these crossings but had refused. The Broadway gate was removed in 1934 to save the company $1,600 a year.

In the 1930s, the economics of transportation changed. With the state building paved roads, trucks could now easily make deliveries and pickups at homes, store or factory. Hubbard's Station closed in 1934 when the Boston and Maine Corporation decided to eliminate the number of rail lines and keep open only the most profitable routes. On July 13, 1953, passenger service from the Broadway station ended. In its place, the railroad company replaced it with a bus route. In September 1980, freight service to Derry was ended. After 131 years, the sound of the train whistle in Derry was heard no more. The tracks were torn up, and much of the rail bed now comprises hiking and biking trails. The depot was sold to become George Grinnell's law office and is now the Depot Steak House.

While trains were excellent at hauling large volumes of freight and passengers, they had certain disadvantages; rail lines were very expensive to

Howard Boyce was the Broadway railroad crossing guard in the decade after World War I.

build and often did not go where you wanted to go. A cheaper alternative to these huge, smoke-bellowing behemoths was the light rail street railroads that are usually called trolleys. The first local trolley line built was the Chester and Derry Street Railroad that had its initial run in September 1896. The forty-five-minute trip between the two towns was over seven and a half miles of track that started at its station near the Broadway railroad depot. It went down Broadway to Derry Village, where, after a few Suzy-Q turns, it went up East Derry Hill and through the woods to the northeast side of Beaver Lake. The rest of the route ran through woods and fields before finally ending at Chester center. The fare was five cents to Derry Village, ten cents to Beaver Lake and twenty cents to Chester.

During the week, trolleys were filled with people going to work or students headed for school. During the weekend, however, ridership sharply declined. To attract more passengers, the trolley company built the Pavilion on Beaver Lake. There, during the summers, was a sandy swimming beach, restaurant, small zoo, slot machines and a dance hall. The Pavilion was destroyed in a 1915 fire and immediately rebuilt but was destroyed again in a 1960 fire. The Chester and Derry Trolley never paid a dividend to its investors and closed in 1928.

The second trolley line was the Derry and Manchester Street Railroad that opened in December 1907. For a thirty-cent ticket you could board the trolley at its office at Broadway and Martin Street and be whisked through the rural landscape of Londonderry and end up on Elm Street in Manchester

The Chester and Derry Trolley in 1896 as it crosses the bridge to Chester Village.

in fifty minutes. A six-hundred-volt current from a Hillside Avenue power station powered the trolley. During the first six months, there were 300,000 paid fares on the line. As automobiles became more common, the number of passengers declined. After years of losing money, the Manchester and Derry Trolley made its last run in August 1926.

Likely the first airship in Derry was that of James Allen Jr., who landed his gas-filled balloon near Broadway in 1892. This aeronaut was flying from Manchester to Newburyport but decided to stop in Derry for lunch. During the town's 200th anniversary celebration in 1919, a plane landed in Hood's meadow, where it got stuck in the mud, and the planned parachute drop had to be cancelled. In 1925, another plane landed successfully in the meadow and offered short rides for five dollars but soon flew away when there were no takers. Some of the locals did take advantage of a similar offer in 1930 during Derry Day at the Manchester Airport in Londonderry. Several residents were flown over their homes in the heated, closed cockpit of a Stinson Cabin Plane.

Derry had a flying club from 1937 until the start of World War II. They had cleared a landing strip on the crest of Ryan's Hill. Their first plane was a secondhand Taylor Craft that was painted gray with red trim. One of their leading members was Myron Smith, who flew four thousand miles to take part in the 1940 Miami Flying Derby. Derry's most famous local pilot was Judge George Grinnell (1910–2000). He had been appointed to the bench in 1951 to replace his father, Herbert, who was retiring. In Derry, his crashes are the stuff of legends. In truth this author has found only three crashes involving the flying jurist: Lake Pawtuckaway, 1961; Beaver Lake, 1962; and near Lake Winnipesaukee, 1988. His first cousin was Alan B. Shepard Jr.

Alan Shepard, after a Derry boyhood, attended the Naval Academy and served in World War II and the Korean War. As a test pilot, he gained a reputation for having ice water in his veins. On May 5, 1961, he became America's first man in space, and the town selectmen proclaimed that May 5 would be "forever" Alan Shepard Day in Derry. Ten years later, he stunned the world by hitting a golf ball while on the surface of the moon. In 1961, the New Hampshire legislature proclaimed Derry to be "Spacetown USA." In Derry, an auto body shop, motel, square dance club and chapter of the John Birch Society used "Spacetown" in their names. The Pinkerton Academy sports teams, which had been called Big Reds, were renamed the Astros after their most famous alum.

The first automobile mentioned in Derry was seen at the Pinkerton Academy graduation in 1899. The first car built in Derry was a mail-order kit model put together by Will Meserve in 1902. It was a two-passenger, four-and-a-half-horsepower vehicle powered by a single-cylinder, two-cycle motor. For many years, Meserve ran the Derry Auto Company from a Franklin Street garage. By 1906, there were 19 cars in town, including 6 Stanley Steamers, 1 Cadillac and 1 Ford. The next year that number grew to 28 autos and 1 motorcycle. In 1923, Derry had 912 automobiles registered, which was the largest number of any town in the state.

The Derry Auto Club was organized in 1916 with fifty-five charter members. Its goal was to promote road safety and campaign for better roads and signs. Each year members would gather for trips to destinations such as the White Mountains or Hampton Beach. In 1916, sixty members gave six hundred local schoolchildren a spin to Windham and back. For many of these children, this was their first ride in an automobile.

The first woman to secure a driver's license was twenty-four-year-old bookkeeper Miss Jessie Anderson in 1907. The first local to drive across the continent was John Kerman, who, with his wife and son, took fifteen days in 1928 to drive to California. The first school driving instructor was Robert Perry, who was hired by Pinkerton Academy in 1953 to teach an eighteen-week course. His 1953 dual-controlled bright green Ford was donated by Watson Motor Sales of Derry.

In 1900, every road in Derry was unpaved. To keep the dust down in the Broadway area, the town sprayed the roads each summer with thousands of gallons of oil mixed with water. It would not be until 1904 that the town began to pave Broadway. The tarring continued at a rate of about a mile per year, so it was not until 1908 that it reached East Derry. It took the state from

Derry's first automobile was built by William Meserve and is shown here driven by local grocer Harry Wilson about 1904.

Members of the Derry Automobile Club at the Oak Street School giving students a ride in 1916.

1916 to 1931 to finish making Route 28 from Salem to Manchester into a cement "truck road." In 1938, the Army Corps of Engineers paved Route 28 Bypass, and the Danforth traffic circle was built to improve the route connecting Manchester Air Field and Fort Devens.

One of the most important events in Derry's modern history occurred in 1931, when the traffic lights were installed at the Broadway–Birch Street intersection. For the next fifty-four years, this traffic light was an important point of reference when giving directions to strangers. In 1985, the town added a second light at the Fordway-Broadway intersection. In 1949, parking meters were installed on Broadway and at first yielded about thirty dollars per day to the town's treasury. They were removed in 1973 after local shopping malls had eroded much of the shopping on Broadway. It was hoped that free parking would lure back most of the business. It didn't.

Before the construction of Interstate Highway Route 93, the north–south route was the slow, twisting course of Route 28 that weaved through the center of many small towns. In 1961, the plans were published by the federal government for a high-speed, limited-access highway that would pass through the western end of Derry. In July 1962, Alan Shepard pushed the button that set off the dynamite charge that started construction on the highway. The section of I-93 running from Salem to Manchester was officially designated as the Alan B. Shepard Highway. This twelve-mile-long road cost just over $9 million and required the construction of twelve bridges and three intersections. It was opened on June 28, 1963, and the road's first traffic accident occurred on that same day. The first fatality was in July 1965.

The effects of I-93 on Derry were dramatic. Derry was now an easy commute to Boston, Lawrence and Manchester. Many wanting to escape the overcrowding and crime in the cities looked to Derry as their way out. Here, the kids could attend the town's excellent schools and grow up in a relatively crime-free environment. Within a decade of the opening of I-93, the town's population doubled, tripled and then quadrupled. Today, Derry's population is five times what it was in 1960.

Derry in 1963 began to attract developers who saw in the town's open land a way to make money. In 1969, a local apartment complex was the largest ever built in the state. A few years later, the Sullivan Corporation proposed to buy the Murdock-White farm on Bypass 28 and built an even larger apartment complex. Many in town, instead, wanted the farm to be converted as a historical-ecological park. This piece of land, with its colonial-era farmhouse, was the site of the common field on which the first settlers planted their first crops. The town meetings of 1974, 1976 and 1977 voted to buy the land to protect it from development, but the budget committee and selectmen thought that the price of $325,000 for 130 acres was too high. One of the town leaders said that apartments are good for the town because they pay taxes and are home to very few school-age children. Soon the Murdock-White home was razed, and the 850 units of the Fairways Apartments were built.

Cartoon showing opposition by local historians to the sale of the Murdock-White farm in 1976. *Illustration by J.E. Kenney,* Derry News.

As soon as I-93 was opened, the traffic in Derry began to markedly increase. For many living in Chester, Hampstead, Sandown or Derry, the road to Route I-93 was right down Broadway. There was no other direct way to get to the interstate. The new apartment complexes, trailer parks and housing developments were home to thousands of commuters that drove through Derry every day on their way to work. In 1964, people were starting to talk about eliminating the Broadway bottleneck by building a Broadway bypass. In 1965, the Derry Planning Board laid out a possible bypass route west from Ross's Corner and entering I-93 at a new interchange called Exit 4A. This proposal was approved overwhelmingly by the town meeting in 1968.

During the next forty years, the battle over Exit 4A continued. In 1988, 1991 and 1992, the legislature and the governor gave the project its encouragement and conceptual approval, as well as ordered the state's department of transportation to work with the two towns to make it happen. Despite these official blessings, the state was frequently opposed to spending money for its construction. On several occasions the project was stymied by federal disapproval of its environmental impact. In 1997, the Derry Town Council voted $5 million to match a similar amount from Londonderry to help pay for the bypass if it ever gets federal and state approval and funding. At the time, it was voted to name the 4A interchange after Derry's former mayor, Paul Collette. In 2008, a nonbinding referendum in Derry voted 1,217 to 1,057 in opposition to spending money on 4A. At present, the cost of 4A is estimated to be $30 million, and it will likely never be built unless federal funding picks up most of the cost.

CHAPTER 7

MILITARY

The town was fortunate in never being attacked by Indians during the eighteenth century. Some have speculated that this was because the Native Americans respected the Scots for not having stolen the land from the Indians; others say the Indians were too scared of the Ulster Scots to attack. Another suggested reason was that the French governor and Reverend James McGregor of the First Parish Church were college friends. The more likely reason is that Nutfield was not on any major river that the Indians could use to paddle their war canoes. In case of attack, however, the town did have garrison houses in East Derry and Derry Village. In addition, a log palisade, or "flankers," surrounded Reverend McGregor's house. He also reportedly brought a gun with him into the pulpit whenever he preached.

During King George's War in 1744, the town bought a barrel of gunpowder, flints and bullets. The next year it bought two more barrels that it stored in the attics of the meetinghouses. Fortunately, there were no lightning strikes! The Londonderry Company consisted of forty mounted soldiers who patrolled the frontier. A number of locals served in the 1745 attack on Fortress Louisburg at Cape Breton Island, including local physician Matthew Thornton.

At the time of the French and Indian War, America's most famous fighting force was the Rangers, led by Robert Rogers, who had once lived in town. His chief lieutenants were John and William Stark, who had been born on Stark Road. One source credits William Stark with showing General Wolfe how to climb the cliffs at Quebec City, which led to the British victory on the Plains of Abraham. The only local man to die during the French and Indian War was William Davidson, who died of smallpox at Crown Point, New York.

During the Revolutionary War, the majority of the residents were aligned with the Patriot cause, but there were a number of locals who remained loyal to the king. Perhaps the most prominent of these Tories was Colonel Stephen Holland, the town's tavern keeper and a selectman. He was, in fact, the leading British spy in New Hampshire. In 1775, the state required everyone except minors, slaves, lunatics and women to sign a loyalty oath, called the Association Test. There were 372, including spy Stephen Holland, who signed the oath and only 15 locals who declined. The leading local Patriot was Matthew Thornton of Derry Village, who has the distinction of being the last signer of the Declaration of Independence.

The records are too fragmented to determine how many locals actually fought in the war. It is known by early 1775 that there were sixty-six in the service from Londonderry, which made the town the second-most patriotic town in the state. In addition to sending our men, we also supported the war through taxes and special assessments. In 1780, the town sent 26,700 pounds of beef to feed the Patriot army. There were three who died in the war: Lieutenant David McCleary, at the Battle of Bennington, 1777; Samuel

Recreation director Jerry Cox was the leader of the Derry Militia during the celebration of America's bicentennial in 1976.

Thompson, of smallpox at Fort Ticonderoga, 1777; and Robert Hunter, at Danbury, Connecticut, 1778.

In the spring of 1775, the word came to town of the impeding Battle of Bunker Hill. Colonel George Reid led seventy locals to stand at the barriers with General John Stark. The town voted to pay these minutemen seven dollars per month. During the battle, the sounds of the canons could be heard in the local area. About this time, rumor spread that the British were attacking the town of Sandown. This led a number of locals to panic. One terrified family hid all night on an island in a swamp near today's Derry-Windham town line.

After the war, the country suffered from severe economic inflation; paper money was nearly worthless and there were almost no gold or silver coins in circulation. Many lost their homes because they couldn't repay their debts. The only ones doing well were lawyers, who were in demand among both debtors and creditors. In 1784, Londonderry passed a resolution that lawyers should cut their fees in half so "they won't be so fond of business and people would have time to breathe." Many were suggesting that the state print lots and lots of paper money that the debtors could use to pay off debts. While the scheme made no economic sense, it was popular with the masses.

In July 1786, a mass meeting was held in a Londonderry tavern to figure out a way to force the state to start printing devalued money. The 150 men from fifteen towns who attended this meeting were described by a lawyer as being of "feeble intelligence." This meeting led to an attack on the state capitol in Exeter by an armed mob in September. The state militia managed to rescue the legislators and dispersed the rebels. Locally, General George Reid arrested Lieutenant John McKeen, who was tried for treason before the Supreme Court, found guilty and kicked out of the army "with ignominy." He was also made to apologize before the town meeting. His grandfather had been the first judge in Nutfield.

Local involvement in the War of 1812 and the Mexican-American War was limited to a few locals being drafted into the army. Probably most tours of duty were spent within the state. There are no known deaths associated with these wars, though Mexican-American War veteran Hiram Rowell of Derry had his health "broken down in the service," but he lived for another thirty years.

During the 1830s, the nation became obsessed with the issue of slavery. The towns of Chester, Auburn, Windham and Sandown all had active antislavery societies; Derry did not. In 1840, several of the state's leading abolitionists tried to hold a rally in Derry but the Congregational, Presbyterian and Methodist Churches refused to allow their sanctuaries to be used for antislavery speeches. The distinguished speakers were taunted by a mean-spirited mob in Derry Village and were soon driven out of town. Later, the town seemed to have become antislavery. In 1860 and 1864, the town voted overwhelmingly for Abraham Lincoln rather than the more pro-Southern candidates.

In the first year of the Civil War, there was considerable support for the war to reunite the union, and thirty local men enlisted in the army. However, as the war continued and the death count mounted, it became harder to fill the town's enlistment quota. Derry began to offer a $300 bounty to anyone who would enlist. Because this proved locally unsuccessful, the town sent an agent to Massachusetts with a satchel filled with money. He was supposed to enlist poor men from cities, but he was soon murdered and the money was stolen.

Nearly two hundred locals served in the army during the Civil War. In addition, an unknown number of non-Derry men served as paid substitutes for local men who did not want to enter the armed forces. There were twenty-five Derry men who died in the war. All the names of the local soldiers are listed on a monument in East Derry that was donated in 1889 by Miss Emma Taylor. Derry was also home to Daniel George and William L.S. Tabor, who won the Congressional Medal of Honor.

The Spanish-American War in 1898 brought about a heightened degree of patriotism in Derry. The wagon of the Nutfield Laundry was painted red, white and blue, and stores gave away silver spoons engraved with Admiral Dewey's portrait and the battleship *Maine*. One brand of whiskey was advertised locally as "Dewey's Eye Opener." There were five locals who served during the war, and when Captain Otis Campbell returned from the front, he was met with a brass band and the firing of a canon.

On the morning of May 3, 1917, most of the town's population mobbed Broadway to see our first doughboys off to fight in World War I. All the factories, saloons, stores, offices and schools were ordered closed for the day. The twenty-eight enlistees were marched to the depot by an escort of honor consisting of the Boy Scouts, Camp Fire Girls, schoolchildren and the Derry Brass Band. Spectators waved hundreds of small American flags as they marched toward the waiting train. At the depot, the soldiers were given coffee and cigars, but the crowd was too thick for everyone to give the young men a farewell kiss or handshake. At 10:15 a.m. the train departed, taking the young men to their fate. What they could not know was that they would all survive and return safely back home to Derry.

Each time a group left for the war, this scene would be repeated, with cigars and coffee being the traditional parting gift before the conductor

Derry's World War I veterans march down Broadway in 1919.

shouted, "All aboard!" Derry would send 290 soldiers to fight in this "war to end all wars." On the homefront, support for the war came via civilians buying Liberty Bonds and stamps at massive rallies. In statewide bond sales, the men, women and children of Derry always met the town's quota. In January 1918, the government saved fuel for the war effort by shutting down our factories for a week and putting them on a four-day workweek until spring. An article in the *Derry News* suggested killing most pets to save food and money for the war effort. The local chapter of the Red Cross sewed thousands of items to be sent to military hospitals. In 1918, there was even a local drive to send tobacco to our men on the front.

The first to die by enemy fire was Lester Chase, who died on May 25, 1918. The Derry Post of the American Legion would afterward be named in his honor. By war's end, there would be fourteen men and one woman who died in the service. That woman was Annie Frasier Norton, a navy yeoman who died of the Spanish flu. She is believed to be the first American woman to die in uniform during time of war. A monument in honor of the World War I veterans was erected at the Adams Memorial Town Hall in 1923. The Veterans Building on Broadway was opened in 1928 as the town's gym and auditorium.

The war ended on November 11, 1918, in a railroad car in France. The news reached Derry by telegraph at 3:00 p.m., and immediately the bell at the Baptist church began to peal. Soon all over the town the sounds of other church bells and factory whistles joined in the jubilation. The schools immediately dismissed the kids, and all the stores and factories closed early. By 5:00 p.m. the newspaper reported that "bedlam had broken loose… everyone went nearly wild." People wept openly and tin plates, cooking pans and cowbells were used to make music in an opportune parade down Broadway. At night everyone gathered around a hilltop bonfire, which was topped with a coffin containing an effigy of the German kaiser.

The Lester W. Chase Post No. 9, American Legion, was chartered in 1919. The General John Stark Post No. 1617, Veterans of Foreign Wars, was begun in 1926. In front of its building a Nike Ajax missile was placed there in 1963. Ninety-eight World War I veterans started the Last Man's Club in 1919. Their most cherished possession was a fine bottle of brandy that they kept in a locked box. It was their intention that the last surviving member would open the bottle and drink a final toast to all his comrades who had passed. In 1975, the last ten members decided that they were becoming too old to continue the club. With the club disbanding, they opened the bottle, poured out ten glasses of brandy and toasted the heroes of the Great War.

During the 1930s, it was becoming obvious that another world war was coming, and the country began to mobilize into Fortress America. In 1938, 1,100 soldiers camped for a night at an English Range Road farm as part of a march from Fort Devens to Portland, Maine. The KlevBro Company on Maple Street was given a contract to make thousands of canvas leggings for the army. In November 1940, the drafting of soldiers began. Carl Thompson, a twenty-nine-year-old father of two children was the first to be called up. He would survive the war. The first local to be wounded in the war was Robert Jodoin, who was hit on December 7, 1941, during the Japanese attack on Pearl Harbor. There were nineteen men from Derry who died in the war.

On the homefront, Derry's citizens once again supported the war effort by purchasing Liberty Bonds. During the first year, the members of the local DAR alone bought $20,000 in war bonds. The local movie house gave free admission to anyone bringing in scraps of aluminum for the war effort. Housewives learned to cook meatless meals; children collected milkweed pods to be put into Mae West–type life preservers for the navy. Our young ladies served as hostesses at a series of dances at the Adams Building for servicemen from the Grenier Air Field. Red Cross volunteers sewed countless bandages. Everyone felt a part of the war effort. Everyone *was* a part of the war effort.

There was a common fear that the Germans would pull a sneak attack on America. On Warner Hill, a round-the-clock observation post was set up to

A Broadway parade in 1942 ended with a rally to sell war bonds.

watch for enemy planes. Civil Defense Corps members patrolled the streets during blackout drills to make sure that all lights were extinguished. The town passed out buckets of sand to homeowners to extinguish incendiary bombs. All of the children were fingerprinted. The war weighed heavily on most civilians because almost everyone had a family member in uniform. It was a total war. Whenever a group of locals would leave on a train for basic training, a group would show them off at the depot with a handshake, cup of coffee and a donut.

News of the Japanese surrender came to Derry via the radio at 7:00 p.m. on August 14, 1945. Immediately, Broadway was filled with celebrants beating five-gallon cans, blowing horns and ringing cowbells as they paraded up and down the street. The sound of church bells and fire sirens added to the din. The next day, a massive preplanned V-J Day parade was held. At night, all traffic on Broadway was halted as the street was turned into a massive block party, with dancing to a live orchestra. In 1949, a monument to the World War II veterans was erected in Pioneers Park; inscribed were the names of the 722 men and women who served Derry.

The next hot war was the Korean Conflict that began in 1950. There were 204 residents credited with wartime service from Derry, and no locals were killed in the conflict. When the war ended in July 1953, there was the usual ringing of church bells but no parade.

During the Cold War, the fear of a Russian attack was on everyone's mind. Starting in 1950, everyone was instructed to listen for "the 5-5-5"—five

Broadway 1942.
*Photo by Arthur
Lear, courtesy of the
Loffler family.*

Broadway, 2009.
*Photo by David
Fuccillo.*

short blasts of the fire siren repeated three times—that would indicate that we were under attack. Schoolchildren drilled on how to crouch underneath their desks if they should see a sudden blinding flash of light. The Plaza Theatre offered free admission for those who wished to see the movie *You Can Beat the A-Bomb*. Many homeowners built bomb shelters in their basements. The town stocked two public shelters with food, blankets and water.

During the Vietnam War, 386 men and women from Derry served in the armed service; four were killed, and one is still listed as missing in action. The war was popular at the beginning, and in 1965 the students at Pinkerton Academy cheered Vice President Humphrey when he announced that the United States must stay in the war. Soon, however, more and more locals

Above: A 1991 parade on Broadway in support of the first Gulf War. Derry News *photo*.

Right: Charles "Cap" Gay (1907–1973) head of the local draft board during the Vietnam War.

began to see the war as being a waste of life. When the war ended on April 30, 1975, the church bells rang for a few minutes, but that was all.

Perhaps the one who fired up the most local antiwar emotion was Charles "Cap" Gay. He was a local political gadfly who would openly brag of "fixing" health violation citations issued to local restaurants. He served many years in the state legislature. In one recent book, he is remembered for getting drunk and bringing a loaded gun into the House, ready to shoot the Speaker of the House. Gay was angry because his usual seat assignment had been changed. Immediately, all of the representatives dived under their seats, and the Speaker hid behind a pile of law books until the state police disarmed Gay. He was chairman of the local draft board, and at an antiwar protest he threatened the attendees by angrily telling them, "I'm on the draft board and I can get everyone of you goons!" In the *Derry News*, he classified antiwar activists as "nuts."

In 1983, a war monument in Pioneer Park was erected to honor those who served in Korea and Vietnam. In 1992, a monument was installed next to it in honor of the 104 veterans of the incursion into Lebanon, Grenada, Panama and the Persian Gulf. The latest war memorial to be erected was unveiled on Memorial Day 2008. It is inscribed with the names of sixty-seven veterans of wars in Iraq and Afghanistan. As this conflict may continue for many more years, there is empty space for future names.

CHAPTER 8

BUSINESS AND COMMERCE

Soon after the arrival of the original Nutfield pioneers, the town's population began to swell with new immigrants. New homes were built, and the original crude log huts were soon replaced. On June 17, 1719, the town leaders granted permission for four men to erect a sawmill on the falls of the lower Beaver Brook in Derry Village. James Gregg was also given permission to build a gristmill in the same area. In 1720, six other men were granted the privilege to start a sawmill at Hood Pond. In exchange for this grant, the men had to sell boards at a price set by the town and "no higher." A fuller's mill was begun in 1728, which was used to clean and fluff linen cloth. By the end of the eighteenth century, about every stream in town was dammed to provide water power for a dozen mills. Most of these mills operated for only a few months each year because of the limited amount of water that could be impounded behind their dams. During dry years, some mills operated for less than a month.

During the eighteenth and first half of the nineteenth century, the majority of the local residents were farmers. As soon as the pioneers arrived, the old-growth forests began to be clear-cut. What the world now condemns in the Amazon, we were doing in Derry 250 years ago. By 1820, the town was likely 80 percent fields, orchards and pastures. This can be easily demonstrated today by hiking onto wood lots far from modern roads. The walker quickly begins to notice meandering stone walls snaking their way through the forests. Such walls are reminders that farming was once practiced in even the most remote parts of Derry. In 1782–83, the town had 283 acres of orchards, 1,325 acres planted in food crops, 2,650 acres in hay or flax and 2,642 acres of pasture; in addition there were 282 horses, 580 oxen and 835 cows.

While family members did most of the farm work, it may come as a surprise to learn there were a couple dozen slaves in town. A half dozen worked at Holland's Tavern, and the rest were scattered across the area, working as farm laborers or domestics. The meetinghouse on East Derry Hill likely had a "slave pen" in the balcony, in which they could sit in a segregated pew. Several of the church's early pastors were slave owners.

Another source of inexpensive labor came from apprentices. An example would be two-year-old Elizabeth Gray, who was taken in by Widow Morrison in 1753. Mrs. Morrison was to provide this orphan girl with board, room, clothing and laundry, as well as teaching her the "trade or mystery of a spinner." In exchange, the girl was to do whatever her mistress required and act "obediently in all things…and behave herself." Boys would usually be apprenticed to learn farming or a craft such as weaving. Occasionally, area newspapers contained legal notices of apprentices running away from their Londonderry master. Publishing such advertisements was likely required to satisfy the terms of the apprentice master's contract. The reward for the boy's return might be as high as six dollars or as low as one cent when the master did not really care if he came back or not.

When the Scotch-Irish finally arrived in 1719, they brought with them knowledge of the weavers trade. Soon, flax plants were growing in Nutfield, and from every house came the sound of the spinning wheel and weaver's shuttle. All over New England, the skill of the Londonderry weavers was well known. The linen was so good that weavers in other towns were selling their inferior cloth and thread and claiming that it was real "Londonderry Linen." In 1748, the town appointed two men as "inspectors and sealers of linen," charged with the responsibility to check the quality of locally produced cloth. Any bolt of cloth that was judged suitable was marked "Londonderry in New Hampshire." It is said that even George Washington and Thomas Jefferson wore clothes of Londonderry Linen. The linen industry seems to have died out locally circa 1800 at the beginning of the Industrial Revolution.

To sell the homespun thread, the young women of the town would frequently walk to Boston carrying as much linen as they could. They would usually sleep at Massachusetts relatives' homes on the first night and arrive in the city on the second day. There, they would trade their linen at a merchant's store for items not available in Londonderry's stores. The women would arrive back home on the third day.

The town's charter of 1722 gave Londonderry the right to hold fairs in May and October. Such fairs were certainly familiar to emigrants from the market towns of the British Isles. While there was a social aspect to such fairs, the main purpose was to merchandize local products. In Londonderry, that meant selling the famous linen cloth and thread. In the open area surrounding William Blake's Tavern and the First Parish Church, long rows of booths and tents were set up by local weavers. Buyers from the eastern cities would flock to the fairground to purchase Londonderry Linen. In addition, out-of-town merchants would bring in cases of items to sell to fairgoers.

Liquor was sold and drunk openly, and the weeklong Londonderry fair had a reputation for being a true Irish donnybrook. Fights were always breaking out between drunken fairgoers. Poet Moses Neal wrote in the *Exeter-Newsletter* about the Londonderry Fair in the 1790s:

> *Two or three bullies stripped to the buff*
> *Two or three noses bloody enough.*

In 1798, the town tried limiting the fair to just two days, closing it at dusk and outlawing the selling of "spirituous or fermented liquor." It seems that these new rules were soon ignored. Doubtlessly many saw the fair as being too profitable to shut down because so many locals made a lot of money selling farm goods and renting rooms to fairgoers. In 1807, there were an estimated ten thousand in attendance each day that the fair was open.

The fair was also famous for its horseracing. The flat stretch on the nearby Lane Road was staked out for a track. Side bets were said to range from hundreds of dollars to as low as a mug of grog. Horse swapping was also a popular fair activity. This occurred when a man with a horse would offer to trade his horse for another man's steed. The two would argue about the weaknesses of the other person's horse, and each owner was expected to lie about the age or condition of his own horse. The deal was struck when one party agreed to give the other man a negotiated amount of money plus his horse in order to get the other man's animal. Dr. Matthew Thornton one year tied his horse to a post outside his office and put out a sign saying, "If you want to trade horse, replace your horse with mine and leave a dollar in the box." At the end of the day, he had twelve dollars in the box and his original horse was tied at the post.

The fair also was like a county fair, with farmers showing off their sheep, cows and oxen. Midway-style tents would exhibit a menagerie of exotic animals including the first African lion ever exhibited in America. In addition, there would be jugglers, pipers, magicians and clowns. One acrobat was billed in the Exeter newspaper as performing feats so amazing that your neck "would be endangered" just by watching her. For many years, one of the performers was a little man who had lost both his legs to frostbite in a snow bank. To the amazement of the fairgoers, he would perform the "pigeon wing" while dancing on the stumps of his legs.

In 1831, the town voted to abolish the fair—believed to have been due to the selectmen voting to abolish all sales of liquor in Derry. Hosting the

Londonderry Fair without hard drinking was thought to be impossible. The fair moved to White's Tavern in Londonderry for a few years and then briefly to the Portsmouth area. The state legislature revoked the fair's charter in 1850.

The first licensed tavern in town was that of John Barr in 1725, though it is likely that William Blake operated one across from the First Parish Church for a few years earlier. In 1730, the town voted to license no more "tippling houses," and in 1755 a petition to the royal government asked that they license no more than three taverns and two stores retailing liquor in town.

Between 1725 and 1768, there were twenty-seven liquor licenses issued from Portsmouth. In just the year 1799, there were nine places in town where alcohol was sold. These taverns were more than just barrooms. They frequently rented rooms and provided meals for strangers, as well as acted as the town's social club and meeting hall. Thom's Tavern on East Derry Hill was our first post office in 1795.

Stores were another source of drinks for the thirsty. The first store was that of Major John Pinkerton (1735–1816) in Derry Village. He started life in Ireland, and as a young man was a backpack trader who would stop at isolated farmhouses exchanging farm goods for hair ribbons, sewing needles and nutmegs. This trading was so profitable that before the Revolutionary War he had built a fine house with one room being used as a store. His brother, Elder James, ran another store one mile away. Both men supplemented their income by loaning out money at interest. The third store was opened about 1774 on East Derry Hill by James McGregor, the son of Pastor David McGregor. Much of the trade in these stores came via the barter system and credit, with little cash being exchanged.

BROADWAY

When the railroad came to western Derry in 1849, there were only five homes visible from the depot. Soon a store, hotel and bank were erected to create a small village called Derry Depot. The name was changed to West Derry about 1900 and then to just Derry in 1907. The first factory on Broadway was the Currier and Boyd Shoe Factory. The enterprise was never successful and soon went bankrupt. After sitting empty for years, a local shoe worker thought he could turn the shoe factory into a profitable business. Because William S. Pillsbury lacked money of his own, he brought in Boston investors to form the Clement, Coburn Company, with Pillsbury as the local manager. Under his brilliant leadership, the company grew beyond anyone's expectations. Soon the factory extended 220 feet along Broadway and 137 feet down Central Street. In addition, there were tenements for the workers and auxiliary structures in which to make shoeboxes and sew buttonholes.

By 1886, the Pillsbury factory occupied fifty thousand square feet of workspace and was producing one million pairs of shoes annually. These shoes came in four hundred styles and were sold on five continents. This annual output more than doubled by 1895. In a town of three thousand residents, he employed seven hundred workers. Of these, 40 percent were women, who earned $1.45 per day, while the men were paid an additional thirty-five cents. There were also employed a large number of adolescent boys and girls, who earned a lower wage. The company closed soon after the death of William Pillsbury and was converted into apartments, which were torn down in 1981.

During the years, other shoe factories came to Derry. The supply of native Yankees, however, was not large enough to satisfy the needs of the expanding shoe factories. The Irish arrived during the 1870s, the French-Canadian about 1900 and the eastern Europeans in the years around World War I. This influx of shoe workers caused a severe housing shortage. Local

Leather sole cutters in the Derry Shoe Factory about 1910.

businesses that wanted this industrial growth to continue formed a building association that built hundreds of working-class homes, several new shoe factories and rows of triple-decker tenements.

The first shoe company to move to Derry was the Perkins, Hardy Company in 1898. This company in 1903 occupied the "Big Shop" on South Avenue, which was claimed to be the nation's largest wooden factory. It was 525 feet long, and its five floors contained almost three acres of work space. Nine hundred men and women worked in that building alone. The building was torn down in 1938, but its 90-foot-tall chimney remained standing until 1976. Just to the east of the Big Shop, the company also operated a 349-foot-long, four-story shoe factory, which was destroyed in a 1915 fire, rebuilt and destroyed again in a 1960 blaze. The Perkins, Hardy also owned three more factories on Maple Street, one of which is still standing in 2009. In 1905, the company employed more than fourteen hundred workers in Derry, who were turning out twelve thousand pairs of shoes per day.

By 1915, an estimated 60 percent of the town's population worked in the shoe factories. The town was pretty much a one-industry town. By and large, the men and women of the town either worked in the factories or in

The Derry Shoe Factory on South Avenue was claimed to be the largest wooden factory in the country. It would go through many owners before being razed in 1938.

the stores and businesses that serviced the needs of the shoe workers. Payday was, by tradition, on Thursdays, and that night the sidewalks of Broadway would be crushed with workers and their families buying things in the local stores, eating in local restaurants or taking in a movie.

Every year, the factories would give the workers a Saturday off with pay. The employees would be taken to a local amusement park for a day's outing. Typical of these outings was that of the Progressive Shoe Company in 1927. The workers and their families were loaded into four busses and fifty automobiles and paraded down Broadway with a police escort and the music of the Derry Brass Band. At Lake View Park in Lowell, the group took part in field games, canoe races, bowling and swimming.

The first modern shoe factory was the brick Crystal Shoe Company that was built in 1927 on Crystal Avenue. In later years, it became the Standard Sash Company and was torn down by 2007. In 1961, the modern 656,000-square-foot Derry Shoe Company was erected at Ross's Corner and employed three hundred workers. Nearby was the equally modern KlevBro Shoe Factory that had been built in 1957. The last three shoe factories to close in Derry were Jodi Shoe, 1969; Derry Shoe, 1981; and KlevBro, 1988. The shoemaking era in Derry had a run of 133 years.

Barry Friedman, the Continental Cobbler, was the last shoemaker in Derry when he retired in 2007.

Cutting ice on Hood Pond in February 1897. In the background is the original St. Thomas Aquinas Church that burned down in 1914. The blocks of ice were transported one thousand feet on a track to the H.P. Hood Co. icehouse.

Perhaps the best-known business from Derry was the H.P. Hood Company, whose dairy products were sold from Maine to New Jersey. Harvey Perley Hood (1823–1900) moved to Derry in 1856 and saw the town's rail connection as a way to link the local farmers to the markets in the cities. Each morning he would sit at a desk inside a boxcar at the Broadway Depot and give local farmers receipts for the milk they sold him. At the station in Boston, he would remain in the car and sell the milk to distributors. On the return to Derry, he remained in the boxcar while he figured out his expenses and sales. He plowed his profits back into the business and kept on buying more farmland, cattle and boxcars.

Soon Hood was selling milk under his own brand name. The Hood Company advertised that it were not just a dairy company—it was a "milk expert." Twice each day, the East Broadway traffic would be halted so the Hood cows could pass between the barn and the pasture. The company's Manning Street creamery turned out over one thousand pounds of butter daily, which was shipped to Boston daily in refrigerated boxcars. Its icehouse measured one hundred by three hundred feet and could hold tens of thousands of tons of ice. It was the first milk producer to guarantee that its dairy products were perfectly safe and sold in sterilized milk bottles.

After the death of H.P. Hood, the company's headquarters were moved to Massachusetts. Hood's Derry Village home is now a Chinese restaurant.

The H.P. Hood farm in Derry Village in 1905.

The company's former pasture is now covered with houses, a golf course, a shopping center and an apartment complex. During the twentieth century the Hood family has given the town a middle school, several parks and a swimming area.

In 1933, Katherine Eastman Hood gave her ancestral home in East Derry to be converted into the Alexander-Eastman Hospital. Additional funds came from a 1920 bequest of Dr. Harrison Alexander. In 1964, the hospital was moved to a new fireproof building at the old circus grounds off Birch Street. In 1983, a new for-profit hospital was built, and the Alexander-Eastman Hospital building was torn down and a medical building constructed on its site.

Originally, the center of town was in East Derry, until in 1806 when the building of the Londonderry Turnpike moved the town's commercial heart to Derry Village. The shoe factories in the early twentieth century made West Derry the most populated part of town and Derry's place to be. Broadway became home to dozens of stores, six churches, several social clubs, a new brick town hall, two movie theatres, many boardinghouses, a library, several drugstores with ice cream counters, many restaurants, a modern fire station and three schoolhouses. Even a few national chains such as the A&P and First National grocery stores, J.J. Newberry's five-and-dime store and the W.T. Grant Company department stores opened on Broadway. The area resembled a small, crowded city with few vacant lots or empty spaces.

The icehouse and creamery of the H.P. Hood Co. about 1900. On the left are the tracks that brought the blocks of ice from Hood Pond.

Former site of H.P. Hood Co. icehouse and creamery in 2009. On the left is the Derry Courthouse and Municipal Center. *Photo by David Fuccillo.*

Emanuel Nelson's store on West Broadway about 1905. Local legend claims that his dairy bar was the birthplace of the ice cream sundae.

Electricity came to Derry in 1891 with the opening of the Derry Electric Light Company. The company prospered and by 1906 had large salesrooms on Franklin Street. In 1913, the company had on display thirty styles of lampshades and four kinds of stoves, as well as vacuum cleaners, roasters, toasters, coffee percolators, foot warmers and curling irons. Soon all of Broadway was lit by streetlights, and the stores had illuminated signs. During the early years, power was cut off at 10:00 p.m. each night and was not reactivated until 6:00 a.m. Electricity came to East Derry in 1918 and to the more rural area by the start of World War II. The electric company went bankrupt during the Great Depression and was taken over by the Public Service Company in 1938.

A century ago, most people in Derry lived and worked within walking distance of Broadway's commercial district. In addition, the two trolley lines allowed easy access to the town from the outlying regions. Derry had now become the market town for all the surrounding towns. The local businessmen's association even set up a room so farmers' wives from Chester and Londonderry could rest after doing their weekly shopping in Derry's stores. Well into the 1950s, the Broadway stores flourished and parking was at a premium, with parking meters yielding a fair profit for the town.

The Subway Café was located on West Broadway in the basement of the Derry Bank. Its clientele was mainly composed of the local shoe workers. It was destroyed in a 1979 fire.

The number of locals who lived near Broadway began to decline in the 1950s because of the equal decline of the local shoe industry. The increase in automobile ownership also meant that workers could drive to work and were not forced to live within walking distance to their employment. The first major store to leave Broadway was the A&P grocery store that moved to Crystal Avenue in 1958. A fire destroyed J.J. Newberry's store in 1963, and the building was never rebuilt. The lot remained vacant for a decade. Soon afterward, the First National grocery store moved out of town to Londonderry, where there was more parking. The Broadway boardinghouses and apartment buildings were by now becoming rather shabby in appearance, and many viewed them as firetraps and slums. The America House Apartments reportedly maintained a jail in the cellar to hold their renters when they came home "too" drunk. The decline of Broadway was obvious to most observers.

In 1963, the planning board hired a town planner to offer suggestions on how to save the downtown area from further decline and economic malaise. He suggested establishing comprehensive, flexible plans. More importantly, he preached that the town needed to set priorities that were achievable. One suggestion from a 1965 planner was to bulldoze most of the buildings, and in their place line Broadway with six-story structures resembling the stark urban architecture found in Russian cities. That downtown renewal scheme was fortunately ignored. In the early twenty-first century, an attempt was made to improve the appearance of the area by having the power and telephone lines on Broadway buried and the sidewalks stamped in a faux-brick pattern.

A devastating blow to Broadway's status as a shopping area came in 1968 when Gilbert Hood Jr. built the Hood Plaza shopping mall on Crystal Avenue. The former cow pasture became home to a dozen stores with acres of free parking. Soon national chains of fast-food restaurants were also being built on Crystal Avenue: Dunkin' Donuts, 1971, and McDonalds and Pizza Hut, 1972; Kentucky Fried Chicken, Wendy's, A&W Root Beer and Taco Bell soon followed these. In 1992, the 115,000-square-foot Wal-Mart store was opened a half mile away from Hood Plaza, and in 1998 another mall was built across from Wal-Mart.

Also in the mall areas was located the Hadco Company, the town's largest employer in the last years of the twentieth century. In 1969, it had built a huge factory on Manchester Road to manufacture printed circuit boards. Soon it was running three shifts and a $25 million annual payroll for its more than 1,400 employees. In 1987, it was listed as America's sixth-largest polluter of the carcinogenic methlene chloride. The company was sold to

Fred E. Stevens at his Railroad Avenue fish store about 1916. *Courtesy of the Stevens family.*

the Sanmina Corporation, which closed the plant in 2002, laying off 450 workers. The building was razed in 2007. Nearby is a sixty-acre industrial park that was begun in 1968 and is now home to a dozen businesses.

The Derry Economic Development Corporation was formed in 1990 with the purpose of helping to improve the economic base of the community. Among its successes include the starting of two award-winning restaurants downtown: MaryAnn's and the Depot Steak House. It also was instrumental in funding the Kendall Pond and Ash Street industrial parks, as well as the commercial building at 6 West Broadway and the former KlevBro Shoe Factory on Manchester Road.

CHAPTER 9

THE POOR

During the early years, the town was a frontier community with few poor but little money. The pioneers ate what they grew and wore what they wove. The first mention of aid to the less fortunate was in 1730 when the town meeting warrant included an article "to see what the town will do about John Moor," who was one of the town's original settlers. At the meeting, the article was "deferred by reason John Moor was dead." In 1744, it was voted to spend no money on the poor. Tough times made for tough decisions. The usual way to handle the less fortunate was to "warn them out." In colonial New England, each town had to support any poor person who was an official resident of the town. A person gained residency by living in a town for more than six months.

As soon as a newcomer arrived, the selectmen would check him or her out. If it appeared that he or she was poor, might become poor, was handicapped in any way, a person of color, had too many children, was a single mother or was elderly, he or she was given an official written order to leave the town within two weeks. A typical "warning out" notice was delivered to Dorcas Billard, a single woman who had just arrived from Boston and was living with Dr. Matthew Thornton. The selectmen determined that she "is likely to become a charge to the town." Dorcas was ordered to "depart immediately out of this town and no longer abide here." During the first century, hundreds of strangers were warned out of town; the last was a group of sixteen who were kicked out in 1806.

In the early nineteenth century, the town dealt with the poor by the "vendue system," in which the care of the poor was sold to the lowest bidder. The winner would provide room, board, bedding and care for a year at a fixed price to the town. In return, the winner could use the poor person as an unpaid servant. An infirmed, bedridden old lady would be sold at a higher bid than a more able indigent person. In 1814, Sally Reid, an unwed mother, and her child sold for sixty-eight cents per week; the more able Nancy Riddle went for twenty-nine cents per week. If, however, the bidder later discovered that poor Nancy couldn't do as much work as anticipated, it was likely that her portions at mealtime would become very small.

In 1784, the town had decided against building a workhouse for "the lazy poor." In the 1820s, the town bought a sixteen-room house and 150 acres of land to serve as a poor farm. Here the indigents would be housed with at degree of dignity at a relatively small cost to the taxpayers. The overseer would make sure that those who could were made to work in the kitchen, fields or barns. Much of the food was grown in its own gardens, and some of the residents were hired out to neighbors to do farm chores. Some families or individuals remained on the farm for over a decade. The farm was sold in 1871 when the county built its own poor farm in Brentwood. The building burned down in 1953 and was later subdivided into 146 house lots called Sunset Acres.

In the decades after the Civil War, the town's welfare costs increased to support the war's veterans, widows and orphans. The annual town report printed the names of everyone who was getting town welfare, such as "75 cents for bed clothes for Albert Redfield" or "$1.25 for a coffin for Allen Menter's child." Any man who received town aid was not allowed to vote in local elections. Another source of aid to the poor came from the "flannel fund," which had been established by the 1870 will of Dr. Sylvanias Brown. Its intent was for poor women to use the free cloth to make clothes for their children. In 1932, the town gave out 2,047 yards of flannel. From 1931 to 1955, the town operated the Hopkins Home on Crescent Street, where elderly women could live with dignity for the rest of their lives for a one-time fee of $1,000.

During the Great Depression, the town of Derry was probably hurt more than any other town in the state. In 1931, a local committee began to collect aid for the poor by sponsoring basketball games, dances and stage shows. Lichtenstein's Department Store donated thirty-two sets of women's underwear, and H.W. Spear gave fifty bags of apples; the Rutter, Benson, Cole, Davis and Head families allowed the unemployed to cut firewood in their wood lots. That year 101 families heated their homes, courtesy of this free wood. Dr. Tappan pledged to care for sixteen poor families, and a number of Broadway stores said that they would give a 10 percent discount to the unemployed.

In September 1932, the town voted to try and borrow money from the state for roads projects. The next month one thousand local shoe workers

Birch Street as photographed from the belfry of the Baptist Church, 1894.

walked off from work because they had not been paid in a month and "were getting desperate." In November, the normally dependable Republican town demonstrated how desperate it was by voting for Franklin Roosevelt for president. His election did bring some hope to the town, and the grange put on the musical *Hello Prosperity*.

The effects of the New Deal's programs soon came to Derry when a few of the unemployed joined the Civilian Conservation Corps. Soon most

Birch Street photographed from belfry of the Baptist Church, 2009. *Photo by David Fuccillo.*

of the local stores were displaying the blue eagle emblem of the National Recovery Administration (NRA). This federal program set rules such as the number of hours that stores had to remain open and rules requiring their clerks be paid a minimum wage of fourteen dollars per week. By the end of the year, there were fifty men in Derry working on federal projects. The government also helped fund a farmers market on Crystal Avenue. Prosperity, however, was not right around the corner, and the school board had to cut its budget by 20 percent. The historic First Parish Church held an emergency meeting in which the members voted to try and keep the church open despite inadequate revenues.

Before the Depression began, the town had a population of about 5,000 residents, with 3,000 working in the town's six shoe factories. By 1935, there was only a single factory still open, and it was demanding that its 1,000 employees agree to a 25 percent pay cut or face closure. Each day there were 500 workers who were traveling up to eighty miles to find work. In Derry there were 825 people on relief, and the unemployment rate was estimated at about 30 percent. In five years the town's spending on the poor relief jumped from $429 to $20,000. In 1935, the three selectmen wrote a letter to the president, begging for more aid, saying, "Our need is great. Don't fail us!"

The appeal seemed to work, and soon seventy-five men were working on a project on Island Pond Road. In Forest Hill Cemetery, more men were employed repairing gravestones; still others were replacing sewer lines or building the swimming area at Hood Pond. There was soon a room filled with women who were hired to manufacture hospital gowns using government-provided sewing machines. A new post office was built on East Broadway, and an artist was paid to sculpt a bas-relief of scenes from Derry's history. The question of whether the New Deal saved America from economic disaster will long be debated. However, what can be said is that here in Derry it gave employment to lots of our unemployed and funded many worthwhile projects.

Since the Great Depression, the town has gone through economic crises every decade or so. Most of these recessions were mild and brief; others were more severe and lasted a couple of years. In 2008, another severe economic crisis hit Derry, and the local unemployment rate is currently around 7 percent and rising. Houses have lost a quarter of their value in only a year's time. "For Sale" signs have sprung up in every neighborhood, but few buyers seem to be buying. In 1999, there were only 3.3 percent of our families living below the poverty level; it is certainly much higher now. In 2009, the town is giving aid to 211 households that consist of 299 adults and 231 children with $124,000 spent on direct assistance. Approximately 54 percent of the aid goes to families with children; only 35 percent goes to single men or women.

CHAPTER 10

THE CHURCHES

The Nutfield pioneers of 1719 were most decidedly Presbyterians. This Calvinistic branch of the Protestant faith was founded in Edinburgh, Scotland, by John Knox (1505–1572). It rapidly became the official church of Scotland and served to unite the Scots against England. In Northern Ireland, the Presbyterians were often punished by the British for their faith, as were the native Irish who were Catholic. Despite suffering for their beliefs, these Scots would never change who they were. The poet John Greenleaf Whittier said that these "stiff necked" Presbyterians "would never give up a pint [point] of doctrine or a pint of rum."

In the first years after settlement, the boundary between church and the state was rather blurred. The town meeting in 1720 voted to build a "small house" to hold both church and town meeting. The site chosen was where the Civil War monument in East Derry is now located. The meetinghouse measured forty-five by fifty-five feet with an interior balcony running along three sides. Lieutenant Governor John Wentworth and his Portsmouth friends paid for some its cost. After the church was built, the pews were auctioned. The winner was given a deed to the pew, which gave him the exclusive use of the pew. As there was no heat in the building, most worshipers in the winter brought with them little pierced-tin boxes in a wooden frame. Inside the tin box was a tray to hold burning pieces of charcoal. In some colonial-era churches, dogs were allowed in as foot warmers.

In time, the local population had grown to the point where a larger meetinghouse was necessary. The committee led by Dr. Matthew Thornton met at Colonel Stephen Holland's tavern to draw up the plans of the new forty-five- by sixty-five-foot building to be built about forty feet south of the old meetinghouse. Its interior was just a single room with a gallery on three sides. The pews were of the sheep pen design, each of which was about six feet square and had a three-foot-high fence around its four sides. Entrance was via a little door that opened from the aisle. These walls helped keep the drafts off the pew owner during the meetings, as well as establishing definite boundaries between pews. The pulpit was raised maybe a dozen feet above the floor. Slip pews for the elders were located directly below the pulpit and faced the congregation.

The erection of the meetinghouse in 1769–70 took the efforts of dozens of men working together. The massive oak frame would be pegged together on the ground and then raised into place by teams of men with long poles, ropes and pulleys. A loud-voiced man would be shouting orders to make sure everyone coordinated their efforts. The town paid for the workmen's lunch of two thousand biscuits, three barrels of rum and five barrels of cider. With all this rum, accidents could be expected. In 1770, a man named Campbell fell to his death from the frame of the meetinghouse.

The Presbyterians' services were very long compared to today's "hour of prayer." On the pulpit alongside the preacher was an hourglass encased in an iron frame. After the first hour of preaching, the pastor would often turn the glass over to give another hour of the Word. Turning it over a third time was not unusual. The long prayer in mid-service consisted of the congregation standing, heads bowed for a half hour. The seats in the sheep pens would fold up to allow the congregation to rest their bodies against the side of the pew. When the prayer was finally over, the pews would be dropped back into place, giving a loud thump that sounded like a hundred trees falling at one time.

Every six months, the church celebrated Holy Communion. These were the high points of the church's year, as Christmas was not celebrated. Ulster Scots from all the surrounding towns would gather to take part in the Lord's Supper. In October 1734, there were seven hundred who showed up for the wine and bread, and the collection that Sunday totaled twenty-five pounds, twelve shillings. It was considered a mortal sin to take communion if one was "unworthy." To keep the undeserving in the crowd from partaking in the Lord's Supper "unworthily," the pastor and elders "fenced it off" by giving out little pewter tokens during the year to those they knew were truly Christian. Each token was marked "LD" for Londonderry. No token, no communion.

On the Thursday before Communion Sunday, there would be a daylong session of lectures and prayer. There would be more prayer on Friday; then on Saturday there would be fasting and more prayer. On Sundays, long tables would be set up in the meetinghouse. On them would be spread snow-white linen tablecloths. The first group of token bearers would be seated at the tables, and the pastor would preach and pray before serving the bread and wine. They would then be dismissed, and the next group would be brought in. It would take all day before everyone had finally been served. It is believed that when weather was agreeable, the tables were set up outside to make it less crowded.

All went well at the First Parish Church under Pastor James McGregor and acting pastor Matthew Clark. When Clark retired in 1732, Thomas Thompson was brought over from Ireland to replace him. By this time, the membership of the church was beginning to change. There were now more Englishmen in the congregation, and they leaned more toward the Puritanical Congregationalism. Conflict began in 1737 when the Reverend David McGregor was ordained. Many in the church felt that he should be made the church's next pastor; after all it was his father, Reverend James McGregor, who had led the Nutfield pioneers from Aghadowey in 1718 and had founded the First Parish Church. The elders instead appointed Reverend William Davidson from Scotland as the new pastor.

After graduating from the University of Edinburgh, Davidson was ordained into the Presbyterian Church. Soon, however, he was refused permission to preach after being accused of being an "Armenian herietick." Armenianism was the belief that salvation came through faith and that a sinner could choose to accept God. The Armenians were accused of believing that sinners were thus saved by their own works. The accepted Presbyterian doctrine was that salvation came as a gift from God and available only through Divine Intervention. Davidson's beliefs, however, were acceptable to the English living in Londonderry but were an anathema to the Calvinist Scots. This theological controversy led to a splitting of the local church.

Those who supported the orthodox Presbyterian preaching of Reverend David McGregor left the First Parish Church and built their own church near today's Pinkerton Academy. In colonial New Hampshire, every resident was taxed to pay for the support of preaching within the community. One's own personal beliefs or lack of beliefs did not matter; the church tax had to be paid. The royal government in 1740 gave permission to divide the town into two parishes with the boundary being a north–south line near where Rote 28 Bypass runs today. If you lived to the west of that line, you lived in Londonderry parish and paid your tax to Mr. McGregor; those in the east or Derry parish paid a tithe to Mr. Davidson. The royal government did permit forty families in each parish to support the church in the other parish. Every Sunday, forty families from McGregor's parish walked past his church to climb the hill to fellowship with Reverend Davidson, while forty families walked down the hill to worship with Reverend McGregor.

This "War of the 40" would continue for decades, with former friends walking past each in silence. McGregor did not seem to personally dislike Davidson, but the same cannot be said of Davidson's feelings toward McGregor. In 1743, when James Wilson asked Davidson for a communion token so he could partake of the Lord's Supper with friends in his old church, Davidson refused, saying, "We admit none that worship with Mr. McGregor." It was only when Wilson promised to "hold not prayer" with McGregor that Davidson gave him his token. In time, McGregor moved his church farther west. That church is now in Londonderry center and is considered the oldest Presbyterian fellowship in America.

During the Great Awakening of the 1740s, the west parish was very much involved in a spiritual revival, and the great British evangelist George Whitefield spoke to a huge crowd in a field near their meetinghouse. The east parish resisted the Awakening and became more aligned with the beliefs of the Congregational Church. While they called themselves Presbyterian, they were rarely involved with the Presbyterian denomination. About 1860, the First Parish Church officially voted to leave the Presbyterian polity because slaveholding Southerners controlled the leadership of denomination.

The First Parish Church building has gone through considerable structural change since its initial construction. In 1824, the whole building was cut in half, and rollers were put under half of the foundation. The eastern end was pulled away by teams of draught animals to open a twenty-four-foot space between the two halves. New construction soon filled in the open space, giving the church two dozen feet of new seating in the auditorium. A Bulfinch-style steeple was added at this time. In 1845, a floor was built across the balcony to create a second floor. The church auditorium moved to this new second-floor space. A low platform replaced the old high pulpit, and "modern" slip pews replaced the box pews. The lower floor became the church's function hall.

An 1822 bequest from Jacob Adams allowed the church to purchase a bell for the church. The bell was believed to have been made by Paul Revere but was recast in 1824 and 1860. This was the first bell in the town and served a number of functions besides just calling the worshipers to church. For many years the town paid a man to toll the bell at 7:00 a.m., noon and 5:00 p.m., making it the town's official timekeeper. The bellman was also paid twenty-five cents to ring the bell at funerals—one toll for every year of the deceased person's life. The tower clock was added in 1880. The Christian education wing and fellowship hall were added in 1973. The carillon was donated in 1974 in memory of Alan Shepard Sr., the church's organist for more than sixty years.

First Parish Church, 1769.

First Parish Church, 2009. *Photo by David Fuccillo.*

In 1834, the First Parish Church lost its preeminence as the only church in Derry. That year the Methodists began holding meetings in Derry Village. The worship services at the First Parish Church were orderly and staid; the Methodists were apt to be more spirit-led. In the East Derry church, the congregation softly sang psalms from Watt's Psalter; the Methodists in Derry Village sang lively choruses that could be heard throughout the village. Soon the Methodists had attracted a large enough fellowship that they could erect their own chapel. A piece of land on Nesmith Street was purchased, and their church home was erected in 1836.

For decades, the Methodist fellowship grew and sponsored many revivals in the town. For many of the more sacrilegious youth, it became almost a rite of passage to attend their spirit-filled meetings and find ways to interrupt the proceedings. Among the usual "tricks" was to put firecrackers into the stove or lure a pack of ill-tempered dogs into the gathering. In 1885, a mission church was begun on Broadway in West Derry. The Derry Village church was torn down in 1927. The mission church, now called St. Luke's, was greatly expanded in 1894 when the whole first floor was raised and a new ground floor constructed.

Derry's third church was the Central Congregational Church on Crescent Street in Derry Village. When it was built in 1837, it was called the First Congregational Church. In 1897, the name was changed to the Central Congregational Church to avoid confusion with the First Parish Church, which had become Congregational. For many years, Central was considered Pinkerton Academy's church. Every year the school baccalaureate services were held at the church, and its pastors were on the academy's board of trustees. It was Pastor Charles Merriam who was instrumental in getting Robert Frost his teaching position at Pinkerton. The church's clock tower and bell were added in 1887. The Hood family donated the stained-glass windows in 1927; the Christian Education wing was built in 1970.

In 1880, the First Baptist Church was formed to bring the Word to the swelling population in the Broadway section of town. Like the nearby Methodist church, it would draw its membership from the area's shoe workers and store clerks. The present building was erected in 1884, and its clock and bell were added in 1887. The Episcopalians began to hold worship services in 1890 and built the Church of the Transfiguration on Oak Street in 1905. In 1960, the Episcopalians built a new church on Hood Road.

As the shoe industry grew in the 1880s, the pool of local workers was soon depleted, and large numbers of foreign workers were soon moving to Derry. The Irish Catholics came first. In 1885, the bishop of Manchester authorized a mission church in Derry. St. Thomas Aquinas Church was

St. Thomas Aquinas Catholic Church and rectory about 1905. The church was destroyed by fire in 1914.

erected in 1888. This structure was destroyed by a 1914 fire and was soon replaced by the present building.

Since the beginning of the twentieth century, the following groups have erected church buildings: First Church of Christ Scientist, 1940; Calvary Bible Church, 1965; Trinity Assembly of God, 1971; Church of the Nazarene, 1910; Church of Jesus Christ of Latter Day Saints, 1989; Etz Hayim Synagogue, 2009; Holy Cross Catholic Church, 2000; and Derry Seventh Day Adventist Church, 1998.

CHAPTER 11

SOCIAL LIFE

The social life of early Derry occurred mainly within the church, school and family with barn dances, cornhusking parties, church suppers, spelling bees and fishing being the most common distractions from the working day. Unfortunately, little was recorded about such frivolous activities. Serious matters such as wars, politics and religious debates get recorded in written histories; fun is forgotten.

We do know that drinking was often times practiced to excess. Foot and horse races are occasionally mentioned. Wrestling was also known to be common. In 1775, John Prentice was not allowed to practice law in town until he grappled with the local champion. He lost the match, but because he put up a good fight he was accepted into the town. There is one story in which a local woman filled in for her absent husband at a wrestling match and threw the challenger to the ground in seconds. At weddings, the shivery, or kidnapping of the bride, goes back to colonial days. Another local wedding tradition was having a horse race, with the winner getting a bottle of rum.

In the early decades of the nineteenth century, a traveling show would occasionally come to Derry. Traveling menageries with a caged lion or an elephant were known to sometimes rent a room at the store or tavern and put on a performance. Because an 1828 town ordinance made juggling, fortunetelling, plays and piping illegal, it is logical that such performers were not unknown in Derry. After the railroad came to town in 1849, performers could get to Derry much easier, safer and faster. Now professionals like Comical Brown would include Derry in their annual tours of the eastern states.

By 1888, Derry had three public venues for shows: Bell's Opera House on Broadway; Association Hall in Derry Village; and the Upper Village Hall in East Derry. Among those who gave public readings in Derry were poets

Comeau's Beach on Beaver Lake during the 1920s was Derry's place to be.

Ralph Waldo Emerson and Will Carlton. Local theatrical groups used the halls for performances, as did national touring companies that presented *Uncle Tom's Cabin* or *Ten Nights in a Bar Room.* Politicians of every shade and persuasion, temperance crusaders and militant suffragettes all used the halls to sell their beliefs. In 1881, one of America's most famous lectures was given in Derry when Russell Conwell delivered his "Acres of Diamonds" speech at the Association Hall.

During the early twentieth century, the most common type of touring performances was the black-faced minstrel show. While today such entertainment is viewed as racist, a century ago they were perceived as inoffensive family fare. Typical was the Sunny South Company that performed in Derry in 1916. The "Kings of Koontown Komedy" advertised the show as "Fun without a blush and Humor without a taint." Local groups also put on minstrel shows to raise funds for their projects. In 1909, the Derry Sons of Veterans offered a black-faced show that "will carry you back to the golden, sunny hours of your youth" with "grins, giggles, tickles, bits of fun and nifty rhymes."

Movies came to Derry in 1907 with a showing at Bell's Opera House of *The Unwritten Law,* based on the scandalous murder of Stanford White by Harry K. Thaw in 1906. The next year a movie of the great Chelsea, Massachusetts fire was shown in Derry only two weeks after the actual fire. In November 1908, the Scenic Movie Theatre opened on Railroad Avenue

Bathing beauty contest at Comeau's Beach in 1939. *Arthur Lear photo, courtesy of the Loffler family.*

with the owner promising a new movie every day. Within days the Pastime Movie Theatre opened on Broadway, offering "movies and illustrated songs" accompanied by the Eagle Quartet, plus live musicians playing the violin and piano. Admission was a nickel.

These small nickelodeons closed after the Broadway Movie Theatre opened in 1913. This theatre could hold four hundred patrons and contained a bowling alley and restaurant. The first "talky" movie came in 1929 with the showing of Al Jolson's *The Singing Fool*. In 1938, it changed its name to the Derry Theatre and became the Plaza Theatre in 1942. On Saturday mornings, the lines of children going to the flickers would stretch down the block. During the Great Depression, promotions such as dish or bank nights filled the seats with paying customers. During the 1950s, patronage began to drop off as people stayed home to watch TV. The Plaza Theatre was heading toward bankruptcy.

In 1966, the theatre owner decided to show "dirty" movies as a way to increase ticket sales. Previously his most risqué movie had been *Peyton Place* in 1958. Now he was showing the European production of *Fanny Hill*. Ticket prices were raised, and entrance was restricted to those over the age of twenty-one. Over the next few years he continued to show family fare such as *Old Yeller* and *The Sound of Music* but tried to offset his losses with the more adult movies.

In February 1970, the theatre became the first theatre in New Hampshire to show the X-rated Swedish film *I Am Curious (Yellow)*. This was, to local moralists, just too much! The Woman's Club presented a petition to the selectmen that had been signed by 236 locals demanding that the theatre not show the movie. In March, the Derry District Court ruled the movie, with its twelve minutes of nudity, to be obscene. The theatre owner was arrested briefly but was soon released. While the case was under appeal, the owner continued showing risqué movies. In 1971, he presented the movie *Female Sexual Emancipation*, but he had it so edited that even the county sheriff found it was not in violation of the state's law on lewdness. The owner also made the theatre a "private club"; to gain admission one had to buy a ten-dollar membership.

In 1972, district judge George Grinnell found the theatre owner guilty of obscenity. He was fined $500 and sentenced to six months in the county prison. The man was released on $2,000 bail. The case was immediately appealed to the state Superior Court, and in time, the charges would be dismissed. The bad publicity had seriously hurt the reputation of the Plaza Theatre. Most locals began to think of it as just a "dirty movie theatre" and a firetrap. The Plaza closed in 1976 and was torn down in 1981. At present the only local movie theatre is the multiplex Flagship Cinemas in a Manchester Road shopping mall.

Until the twentieth century, the most exciting holiday was Independence Day and not Christmas or New Years Eve. At midnight on July 3, gangs of local youth would find ways to sneak into churches and ring their bells until everyone in the neighborhood was fully awake and irritated. At daybreak, a "horribles" parade of children in weird costumes would snake through the villages while beating on tin pails and blowing horns to awaken the adults. During the day, local politicos would give long patriotic orations. A Civil War veteran wearing the blue uniform of the Grand Army of the Republic (GAR) would be invited to give a speech about the war. Many times children would giggle when the old gray-bearded man began to cry while reminiscing about former comrades so many years dead. Firecrackers were sold openly, and many a town father had to do an impromptu dance when a string of Chinese Crackers was lit under his feet. At night a bonfire was burned on top of a local hill.

During the first three quarters of the nineteenth century, there were only a few social clubs in Derry. The first fraternal organization was St. Mark's Lodge of Masons that was started in East Derry in 1826. The Derry Historical Society first met in 1855. After the Civil War, there were two local posts of the Grand Army of the Republic, each with its own women's branch. The Nutfield Grange began in 1874 as an organization to improve the lives of farmers. The rapid growth of the local shoe industry caused a huge swelling of the population of West Derry. These factory workers put in fifty-five hours a week at work and so had considerable free time left over after sleeping and eating. Some spent their off hours in the local saloons; others elected to meet in social, fraternal, religious or sports clubs.

The period from 1875 through 1925 was the golden age of clubs in Derry. Every year there were formed new men's and women's groups. Some of these were national organizations like the Odd Fellows (1879) or Rebekahs (1881); others were strictly local such as the Donna Club (1890), which consisted of women who worked in the shoe factories. Some of these would survive only a few years such as the Order of Brit-o-Mart (1889–93); others have been meeting in Derry for many decades such as the Halcyon Club (1913) and Molly Reid chapter of the Daughters of the American Revolution (1894).

Perhaps the most spectacular local fraternal group was the Hammonasset Tribe #34 of the Improved Order of Red Men (1901) and the sister group, the Neoskaleta Council #18 Order of Pocahontas (1904). Together they had about two hundred members and met twice a month at the Odd Fellows Building. They claimed to be the descendants of the "Indians" who threw the tea into Boston Harbor during the Revolutionary War. Each year they would have a fair that attracted several thousand paying guests. In 1903, the Red Men's fair included the reenactment of the "burning of a pale face at the stake," a parachute drop of a man from a hot air balloon and a bareback horserace. In 1908, their state convention was held in Derry, and the town was treated to the sight of hundreds of Red Men marching down Broadway while wearing huge feathered headdresses, bejeweled tunics and red sashes. The Red Men and Pocahontas organizations died out by the 1920s.

For the first couple of centuries, the children of Derry were usually allowed to organize their own free time without the control of adults. While there were church groups and Sunday schools, most of the time after school and chores were completed was their own. The first known national organization to try and harness our free-range kids was the Boy's Brigade that began at the Central Congregational Church about 1908. Their members wore a blue military-style coat with brightly polished brass buttons with a sword hanging from their belt. They were advertised as being both a religious and military organization to promote "Christian manliness."

The Derry troop of the Boy Scouts of America founded in 1914 was the first in the state, thus it was labeled Troop #1. At its first field day, scouts used signal flags to send the message "Glory be to God" to another team a quarter-mile away. Benjamin Adams in 1933 allowed the scouts to build

Astronaut Alan B. Shepard Jr. and family during a Broadway parade in 1962. *F.J. Sullivan photo,* Derry News.

a log cabin on his land. To get access to the site they had to blaze a mile-long trail through the woods and build a corduroy bridge through a swamp. Because they accidentally settled on the wrong piece of land, it was called Camp Mistake.

The first known girls' organization was the Tsienneto Camp Fire Girls, which began at Pinkerton Academy in 1915. Among its charter members was Renza Emerson, the mother of Alan Shepard. According to the local newspaper, they reportedly enjoyed "boating and tramping." The Girl's Club came to town in 1921 and the Girl Scouts in 1932, which was divided into the Butterfly and Moccasin patrols. The Girl Scouts proved so popular that soon it was necessary to split in two troops, sponsored by the American Legion and First Parish Church. During World War II, the Boy and Girl Scouts helped the war efforts by collecting scrap metal, selling war bonds and acting as runners during air raid drills.

Perhaps the youth group with the most unusual name was the Ocean Born Mary Chapter, Children of the American Revolution, which met in the 1960s. The Boys Club in 1981 was offered twenty-two acres of land on East Derry Hill for a clubhouse. The donor, Maury Needham, president of Hadco Corporation, placed one restriction on the gift; the group had to change its name to the Greater Derry Boys and Girls Club. The world champion Red Star Twirlers began in 1976 and under the leadership of Gina Hutchinson have traveled throughout the world. Many of the girls have gone on to twirl at major colleges. Various youth drum and bugle corps and marching bands have been formed locally. John and Bill's Diner sponsored the first in 1931. The next year, renamed the Derry Junior Drum Corp, they won the New England championship. The Spacetown Cadets marching band was a regular feature in local parades and presidential campaign rallies in the 1960s.

The first non-schoolchildren's sports team was likely the Derry Little League that was organized in 1953 with four local teams in the rotation. Today there are 700 kids playing in the Little League program in addition

Gail Wilson, a member of the Derry Timberwolves, does the running long jump at a 2003 meet in Hudson. *Photo courtesy of the Derry Recreation Commission.*

to 152 in girls' softball and 165 very young players in "Grasshopper" baseball. Also in 2009, the town has seven Little League regulation-size baseball fields, one full-size softball field, one full-size baseball field, ten multipurpose soccer/lacrosse fields, two beaches, one dog park and five tennis courts. The Derry Soccer Club offers the sport to 459 players. The Derry Demons have 250 football players and cheerleaders in their program. There are also 186 playing in the youth lacrosse and 901 young adults in town-sponsored baseball.

The adult sport club that brought the most attention to the town was the Derry Athletic Association, founded in 1904. Their semipro baseball team was considered the powerhouse of southern New Hampshire. Two of its members, brothers George "Lefty" and Fred "Casey" Tyler, played for the Boston Braves of the National League. The DAA would frequently play exhibition games with touring professional teams. In 1922, they beat the House of David before two thousand paying spectators. The *Manchester Union Leader* reporting on the game said, "And it came to pass that thee sons of David descended upon the Philistines in their stronghold in Derry. And the Philistines arose and smote the sons of David hip and thigh. As so there was peace in the land." During the winter the DAA fields on South Avenue were flooded for ice-skating.

The most popular activity sponsored by the DAA was the annual winter carnival, which was held from 1924 through 1953. Thousands would attend the parade, coronation ball for the carnival queen and vaudeville shows. Among the carnival's sporting events were races on skis, skates and snowshoes. In 1925, the DAA added a 25-foot-foot-high ski jump at the site of today's Exit 4 of I-93. The jump was later rebuilt at Birch Street's Alexander-Carr Park. In 1964, recreation director Jerry Cox began constructing a new ski area at this park, which featured a 620-foot-long rope tow. Local teenagers were recruited for the ski patrol. The next year, Cox began offering ski lessons for housewives. The rope tow would eventually be shut down, partly because of insurance considerations.

Today's equivalent of the winter carnival is the Frost Festival, which began in 2000. It features wintertime athletic contests and a formal ball. Among the other long-running events was Laborfest, which was held every Labor Day weekend from 1964 through 1971. In 1965, an estimated thirty thousand attended its parade and field events, which included a beauty contest, stage show by TV star Rex Trailer and helicopter rides. Derryfest at Pioneer Park has been held every fall since 1990.

The local organization that gained the most international fame was the Derry Driving Club, organized in 1938 to race horses on the ice at Beaver

The queen and her princesses parade down West Broadway during the 1925 Winter Carnival.

Racing on ice on Beaver Lake, 1939. The driver on the right is George Grinnell, a future judge of the Derry District Court. *Courtesy of the Loffler family.*

Lake. Its best-known members were blacksmith Charlie Doherty and District Judge George Grinnell. Racing on the lake had been practiced informally as far back as 1923. To give the horses traction on the slippery track, the horseshoes were fitted with special spikes called caulks. Starting in 1937, the races were filmed for movie newsreels that were shown all over the world. Many local World War II soldiers reported seeing movies of the races while on both the European and Pacific fronts. At times nearly two thousand spectators were on hand to watch the horses fly down the half-mile track. The last race was held in 1954 with a dozen sulky riders ranging from ages ten to eighty-seven. Private wagering among the spectators was common.

CHAPTER 12

COMMUNICATION

During the first century after the town's first settlement in 1719, most locals would go through their entire life without receiving any mail. Merchants, lawyers and the clergy would occasionally get letters, but not the average man. Most locals had little real need or interest in corresponding with those beyond the immediate area. The postal system was also too chaotic for letters to have any certainty of arriving in a timely manner. A letter sent home by a Revolutionary War soldier might take more than a month to arrive back in New Hampshire even if it was given to a friend who was heading that way anyway. Postal service to Europe or between coastal cities was fairly reliable; mail to rural New Hampshire was not.

The town's first post office was opened in 1795 during the administration of George Washington. It was located at the tavern of Dr. Isaac Thom, which was diagonally across from the First Parish Church. The post rider would drop off letters at the tavern, and Thom would hold the mail until it was claimed. The letter might sit at the tavern for weeks. A weekly newspaper was regularly delivered to Thom's Tavern. It would be brought to a loud-voiced church elder who would position himself under an oak tree near the church. A crowd would gather around him as he read out loud the entire four-page *Portsmouth Gazette*, including advertisements and legal notices.

For a century, the position of postmaster was a political appointment. A newly elected Republican president would throw out the incumbent Democratic postmaster. ("To the victor go the spoils.") It was only after the introduction of the Civil Rights Act of 1883 that such appointments ceased to be a political plum. After 1795 the local post office moved eighteen times. In 1817, the post office was moved to Derry Village but was moved back to East Derry and after only six months was transferred back to Derry Village, in which, during the next seventy-five years, it moved five more times. In 1907, the post office moved to Broadway. Since then it has moved ten different times but has remained on Tsienneto Road for the last decade. The home delivery of mail began in 1903 with five mailmen on horseback covering a seventy-six-mile-long route.

Just before the Civil War, the telegraph arrived in Derry with its office located at the Broadway depot. Now the residents could have instantaneous access to the larger world. During one week in 1881, the local office was connected with eighty operators in twelve different states. In 1877, the Chester and Telegraph Company was formed with officers in Derry Village. A message from Chester would be received there and resent on another line to the Broadway depot, where that telegrapher would send it out on the American Telegraph Company trunk line. In 1908, a private line was strung to the Odd Fellows Building on Broadway where, for twenty-five cents, one could get the presidential returns as they came in from across the nation.

The first telephone line was strung in Derry in 1880, and the only telephone was located at the Broadway railroad depot. The local newspaper correspondent likely echoed the sentiments of many when he wrote that the poles and lines were "not very ornamental to say the least." In 1882, milk king H.P. Hood paid for a private line to be strung from his Derry Village home to the depot. Soon others were paying three dollars to buy a telephone receiver, and a local telephone company was formed. To make a call one would turn the crank to be connected to the "Hello Girl" at the switchboard at the Odd Fellows Building. The caller would tell her the name or number of the person one wished to speak with, and she would make the connection. Later, as more locals began to subscribe for telephone service, the list of individual telephone numbers began to grow longer, reaching four digits by the late 1920s.

In 1930, there were 1,050 telephones in Derry and an estimated 6,000 calls being made every day. Of these, only 350 calls were being made to out-of-town locations. To handle all this telephone traffic, a new up-to-date exchange was built on East Broadway. Now all the customer had to do was lift the receiver off the hook, and the operator would respond with "Number please." In previous years, the operator would tell the customer if the line was busy. Starting in 1930, customers would be informed that the call could not go through by the now ubiquitous "busy signal." Additions to the original beige-colored stucco building were added in 1969 and 1973.

Having a live local operator was considered a benefit to many residents. People asked the operator for the correct time, if the school was having a snow day or the amount of time needed to cook a turkey. As Derry grew, there became the need for a more modern telephone system. By 1960, the number of subscribers had doubled in just fifteen years. In May 1961, the town went to a dial system with the local exchange being designated as Hemlock. My telephone number in Derry would have been He4-6042. When the telephone company became digitized, that number would have evolved into 434-6042. Originally, all calls outside of Derry were toll calls, but in 1966, in exchange for a higher monthly bill, the free calling zone was extended to include thirteen surrounding towns.

During the 1990s, the number of hard-wired home telephones began to decrease as more residents began to purchase cellphones. To handle this wireless calling, a 180-foot-tall communication tower was built in 1998 in the center of historic Derry Village. Its erection was approved without public input by a 5 to 1 council vote. Only Jim MacEachern voted against the tower. Councilor Gordon Graham later admitted to the *Derry News*, "It was not at all what we thought it was going to look like." All that Town Administrator Earl Rinker could say was, "It sounded like a good idea at the time." Arts council leader Elizabeth Ives commented, "It's extremely ugly…It's just a stupid place to put it," and businessman Troy Allen added that it was "the most God-awful thing ever built!" Now, more than ten years later, the tower still stands, but most locals have learned to ignore it and legal restrictions are now in place to prevent future towers from being erected without public hearings.

The first radio in Derry was installed in 1921; within months there were a dozen sets in town. Within a decade about every home in Derry was listening to music, soap operas, situation comedies and church services over the air. This free home entertainment was a key factor in the decline of the town's social clubs and organizations. Some locals, however, were afraid that the broadcasting of invisible radio waves through the air would disrupt the weather and cause either drought or torrential rains. Starting in 1924, the returns from presidential elections were broadcast to politically minded citizens. In 1926, hundreds of locals reported hearing the Tenney-Dempsey boxing match broadcast from Philadelphia. Derry's first and only radio station is AM 1320 WDER, which received its license in 1981.

The first locals to experience television are believed to be Mr. and Mrs. Donald Houston, who were broadcast by an experimental station at the 1939 New York World's Fair. For another decade, however, TV remained only a futuristic dream. When the first New England television station was opened in Boston on June 4, 1948, there were exactly three television sets in Derry. That night at the home of Arthur Levesque, there were fifty adults and children crowded into his living room. They all sat mesmerized by the snowy picture on the tiny screen. Other crowds were also gathered in the

Broadway stores of Arthur Bertrand and Clarence Gallien. Soon all over town, silver-colored metal antennas were being fastened to chimneys. Those antennas would start to be removed in June 1971, when cable television began to be offered in Derry.

Derry's first television station began broadcasting in September 1983 as Channel 50 WNDS-TV, "the winds of New Hampshire." During its first years, it broadcast local news, as well as live children and adult shows from its studio at the Manchester Road industrial park. These shows and most news broadcasts ended in 1986, but the flamboyant weatherman Al Kaprielian was kept on. In 1997, the station was sold to a home shopping network, which turned channel 50 into a twenty-four-seven advertisement for jewelry, clothes and glitzy knick-knacks. This network failed to actually buy the station, and WNDS soon reverted back to its original owners. In 2004, the station was sold to Shooting Star Broadcasting Corporation, which changed the station's name to WZMY-TV and became affiliated with MyNetwork TV.

The town's second television station began in 1990 when Mike Henson and Jon Kissel persuaded the cable company and the town to support a local public access station. Originally called Channel 38, it was soon broadcasting meeting of the town council, planning and zoning boards. In time, many locals and even Santa Claus would have their own shows. The station, now named Channel 17, currently operates under the direction of Barbara Ellingswood. Local parades, special events, musicians, exercise classes, school announcements and historical tours are frequently shown on the popular community bulletin board. There are also cable stations at the public schools and at Pinkerton Academy.

In recent years, more and more information comes to us via the Internet and the World Wide Web. The first known local use of computers was believed to have occurred in 1971, when Pinkerton Academy purchased a Wang 5000 for $3,000. At the time, there were only two other school-owned computers in the state. Eight students were selected to take lessons from the Wang Corporation, and the *Derry News* reported that "soon the teenagers were teaching the Academy's business manager how the computer could be used in his office." This machine amazed everybody by being able to perform a sixty-four-step program. By 1984, there was one computer for every sixty-one students in the Derry School District. It would not be until 1989 that school grades were computerized. Soon, however, many bugs were discovered in the program, and the first semester report cards at Hood School were sent out a month late. By the second term, things got better and they were only a week late. The kids never complained.

BIBLIOGRAPHY

Bolton, Charles Knowles. *Scotch Irish Pioneers in Ulster and America.* Boston: Bacon and Brown, 1910.

Browne, George Waldo. *Early Records of Londonderry, Windham and Derry, N.H., 1719–1762.* Town clerk's records. Manchester, NH: John B. Clarke Co., 1908.

Cummings, O.R. *Trolleys to Beaver Lake.* Forty Fort, PA: Harold E. Cox, 1990.

Daniel, Jere R. *Colonial New Hampshire.* Millwood, NY: KTO Press, 1981.

Derry Historic Research Committee. *From Turnpike to Interstate.* Canaan, NH: Phoenix Publishing Co., 1977.

Forsaith, Carl Cheswell. *Pinkerton Academy 1814–1964.* Derry, NH, 1965.

Glazier, Michael. *The Encyclopedia of the Irish in America.* Notre Dame, IN: University of Notre Dame Press, 1999.

Hitchcock, Edward. *The Life and Labors of Mary Lyon.* Northampton, MA: Hopkins, Bridgeman and Co., 1852.

Parker, Reverend Edward L. *The History of Londonderry.* Boston: Perkins and Whipple, 1851.

Pillsbury, Parker. *Acts of the Anti-Slavery Apostles.* Concord, NH, 1883.

Bibliography

Upton, Richard Francis. *Revolutionary New Hampshire*. Hanover, NH: Dartmouth College, 1936.

Willey, George F. *Willey's Book of Nutfield*. Derry Depot, NH, 1895.

Newspapers

Derry (NH) *News*: 1880–present
Evening Record, Derry, NH: 1919–33
Exeter (NH) *News-Letter*: 1831–80
New Hampshire Gazette, Portsmouth, NH: 1756–1831

Manuscripts, Public Documents, Collections and More

Derry Heritage Commission. Inside its museum and research library (29 West Broadway, Derry, New Hampshire) is a large collection of diaries, scrapbooks, newspaper clippings, photographs, maps, postcards and manuscripts relating to all aspects of the town's history.

Derry Public Library. Microfilms of area newspapers and maps within the library's collection.

New Hampshire Historical Society, Concord, New Hampshire. Here is housed a terrific collection of books, maps and manuscripts relating to Derry.

New Hampshire State Archives. The earliest manuscript town records of the Nutfield towns are stored within its huge collection.

New Hampshire State Library, Concord, New Hampshire. Here can be found microfilms of the state's earliest newspapers and records.

Provincial and state papers. These thirty-four volumes were printed by the state during the nineteenth century and contain a vast amount of official records relating to the area in the eighteenth century. A complete set can be found at the Derry Public Library.

Taylor Library, East Derry. This library contains excellent records relating to the Adams Female Academy.

Town clerk's records, Derry, 1827 to present. These records are stored at the town's Municipal Center.

Town of Derry, New Hampshire. Annual Reports, 1836 to present.

In addition to these sources, the author has for many decades spent countless hours in private conversation with former and current town officials, as well as many private citizens of Derry.

Visit us at
www.historypress.net